What

The essential
over 500 popular children's foods

Clare Panchoo

First published in Great Britain in 2008 by
Virgin Books Ltd
Thames Wharf Studios
Rainville Road
London
W6 9HA

A catalogue record for this book is
available from the British Library.

ISBN 978 0 7535 1363 7

Mixed Sources
Product group from well-managed
forests and other controlled sources
www.fsc.org Cert no. TT-COC-2139
© 1996 Forest Stewardship Council
FSC

Typeset by Palimpsest Book Production Limited,
Grangemouth, Stirlingshire

Printed and bound in Great Britain by CPI Bookmarque, Croydon, CR0 4TD

Contents

Contents

Acknowledgements

First and foremost, I would like to thank Emma Izaby who had the original idea for the A to Z reference guide and asked me to write it. I would also like to thank all those mums who have shared with me their concerns about feeding their children and all those mums who helped me with planning this book and in deciding which foods I should analyse.

I would also like to thank Carolyn Thorne and Gareth Fletcher at Virgin Books and my agent Rob Common for all their help and for making this book a reality. A huge thanks to my dear friend and excellent nutritionist, Sarah Queen, whose help in editing the book was invaluable. Many thanks also to Helen Conn, one of the country's leading food scientists, who helped me decipher the sometimes very technical terminology found on ingredients lists.

Lastly, I would like to thank Jazz, my husband, and Zara, my two-year-old daughter, and my parents for their support and understanding as I juggled family life with book writing.

About the Author

Clare Panchoo (née Dodgshon) MSc. graduated in 1994 with a masters degree in Human Nutrition. She has spent the last fourteen years practising as a nutritionist helping many hundreds of clients and giving nutrition lectures in schools, health clubs and large corporate companies. She has advised a number of large coffee shop chains, cafes, restaurants and food producers on labelling, helped them develop healthier products and healthier choices on their menus and write customer information leaflets. Clare is also regularly asked to contribute to TV and radio discussion programmes, magazines and national newspapers on nutrition issues.

She lives in Oxfordshire with her husband and their two-year-old daughter, and their second baby is due spring 2008.

About What's in This?

What's in This? was co-founded in 2007 by Emma Izaby and Clare Panchoo. One day whilst feeding a well-known children's yogurt to two of her many nieces and nephews, Emma looked at the ingredients list and, when she struggled to decipher what half of the words meant, she saw a need for a reference guide to help parents discover what was in the foods they were feeding their children. Emma approached Clare Panchoo, a qualified nutritionist, with the idea and together they have worked hard to make it a reality. They are now working on developing a series of books under the What's in This? brand.

Foreword

By Dr Jonty, star of BBC1's *Street Doctor*

Everyday there is another story in the media about what we should or should not eat. We are bombarded with information from every direction. This should allow us to make the best possible choices for ourselves and our children. Unfortunately, far from empowering us to make healthy choices, most of us feel overwhelmed by what is often conflicting and needless detail.

The beauty of this book is that it gives parents all the important information they need to make healthy decisions for themselves and their children, and it does this in an easy and accessible way. In a world where we are increasingly reliant on pre-prepared food, it is essential to understand what is in what we eat, and what we are feeding our children. This book is an essential reference guide for any busy parent who is concerned to give their child the healthiest start in life.

chapter 1

Why I Put Pen To Paper

The first fact I discovered when researching this book is that no special legislation exists for foods and drinks aimed at children over twelve months of age. This means any food we feed our children beyond this age, which is not specifically a weaning food, is not subject to any different legislation than adult foods. So, though a food may be produced for and marketed at children, there are no specific limits on the levels of salt, sugar and fat it can contain. It may also contain any number of over 500 additives.

It is increasingly unrealistic to avoid giving your child any 'processed' foods. The fact is, parenthood can often be hectic and exhausting, and relying on ready meals from time to time is only natural. Even when, as parents, we manage to cook many of our child's meals from scratch, there will be some basic processed staples which will be part of every child's diet, such as breads, breakfast cereals and fruit yogurts, all of which have been processed in some way and contain a mix of ingredients and additives.

Having practised as a nutritionist for well over ten years before I became a mother for the first time, I have to admit that, though I had always been passionate about food and interested in the positive and negative effects it can have on our health, I had not really taken very much notice of the whole area of children's foods. This changed the day I began weaning my daughter.

Feeding your child a balanced diet can sometimes feel like a huge and quite daunting responsibility. It is in early childhood that eating habits and tastes are developed that will last their whole lifetime and the building blocks for their long-term health are laid down. As a parent myself, I soon realised that there can be many day-to-day struggles in trying to get a child to eat a healthy and balanced diet: such as how difficult it can sometimes be to actually get a toddler to stop playing and sit down to eat anything at all, the battles when trying to get fruit and vegetables into a child's mouth and how it can sometimes seem like a huge achievement just to get them to try a new food.

As my daughter began to eat a greater variety of foods, I took an increased interest in the ever growing number of products in supermarkets aimed specifically at children. I began reading food labels and taking a real interest in the ingredients lists, the nutritional information and how these foods are marketed.

I am often asked by other mothers what I feed my daughter or whether something is really bad for their child to eat. I usually answer that, as a family, we try to live by the 80:20 rule. Eighty per cent of the time we eat a healthy and balanced diet, but as food is one of life's great pleasures we also eat a little of what may be regarded as 'naughty'. I follow this rule with my daughter and think that, in part, her love of food comes from the fact that I have strived not to be overly strict. The simple fact is, it is never one food which affects our health, but rather our overall diet. Therefore, it is not a food eaten occasionally which will have most impact on our children's health but foods which they are eating more frequently or daily. These foods will have a much greater impact on their long-term health, as well affecting their energy levels and their ability to concentrate, to play and to sleep.

As parents we are often overloaded with advice, so I wanted to avoid writing a book that in any way dictated what you should be feeding your child or added to the pressures and guilt of parenthood. Instead, I hope that you will use this book as a reference guide to help you make an informed choice about what foods you feed your child. You will all have some basic concerns as parents, but each of you will also have more specific concerns for your own individual child. This book will hopefully arm you with the basics you need to know when assessing how suitable a food is for your child as well as providing more in depth information should you want it.

WHICH PRODUCTS DID I ANALYSE?

I looked at a total of 570 products: 563 foods and drinks aimed specifically at children or those staple products which children may be eating regularly.

The foods were sourced from ten major supermarkets and include a mix of own brand foods, economy brand foods and well-known branded foods, as well as a selection of smaller brands and new brands which have developed ranges of foods aimed specifically for children.

The foods I looked at included a range of what may be described as 'healthier' meals, drinks and snacks as well as some of the staple basics (bread, breakfast cereals, spreads) and a range of popular processed children's foods, for example chicken nuggets and burgers, lunchbox products, yogurts, confectionery, savoury snacks and a wide range of soft drinks. I also looked at a range of tinned foods, frozen foods and fresh foods. Products included vegetarian ones, gluten free ones and also some of the weaning foods and cereals aimed at infants and young children.

I also looked at a selection of seven different children's medicines.

HOW DID I CHOOSE THE PRODUCTS?

I based the choices on a combination of the following:
• Were they well-known products eaten and loved by children on a daily basis?

- Did the packaging target children?
- Had they been advertised to children before, on TV, magazines, posters or through school projects?
- Had I seen the products written or talked about by the media in newspapers, magazines, or heard them on the radio or seen them on TV?
- Were they simply a 'mum's favourite' due to the history/heritage of the product?

WHY DO I NOT LIST THE PRODUCTS?

Ingredients in foods can change rapidly. This especially occurs when new legislation is introduced. Therefore, I felt it was more sensible and useful to create an A–Z of the most popular ingredients used by food companies. You can then use the A–Z list to cross reference with any product.

HOW TO USE THE GUIDE

The guide is designed to be used again and again as a quick reference guide in your kitchen or as a handy reference shopping guide.

Find Out About An Ingredient On A Packet In Your Kitchen

Step 1: Start with a food that your child regularly eats in your cupboard or fridge. Have a look at the ingredients list.

Step 2: Are there any ingredients, additives or strange sounding words which you have no clue what they mean but would quite like to know as your child is eating them? Look up the ingredient in the alphabetical A–Z reference (Chapter 6: A–Z Reference Guide) in this book for a simple, non-technical explanation.

Step 3: If the ingredient is listed only with its E number then look up the name in the Complete E number list (Appendix 1: Information on Additives) and then you can look the name up in our reference guide (Chapter 6: A-Z Reference Guide).

Step 4: Chapter 7 provides a simple overview of all my findings for each product range and highlights the key things to be aware of when choosing foods.

Want To Know Even More?

Step 5: If you'd like to be better informed to make choices when shopping or planning meals then read:

- Chapter 2: What Every Parent Should Know About Food Labels
- Chapter 3: What Every Parent Should Know About Children's Nutrition
- Chapter 5: Manufacturers' Claims: What Do They Really Mean?

Step 6: If your child suffers from asthma, behavioural problems or skin sensitivity turn to:

- Chapter 4: Adverse Reactions to Foods, for some advice about avoiding foods which have been linked to adverse reactions in sensitive children.
- Chapter 6: A-Z Reference Guide. You will also find some information within the guide listed under specific ingredients or additives. You can also make a note of any additives you may wish your child to avoid by listing them on the pages at the end of the A-Z Reference Guide.
- Appendix 2: Further Useful Information
- Appendix 3: Useful Contacts and Further Information Sources For Parents

chapter 2

What Every Parent Should Know About Food Labels

OVERVIEW

UK food labelling is based on requirements set out in the Food Labelling Regulations 1996. Some foods also have additional labelling requirements specific to them, and a set of regulations exists for each of these.

However, whilst there are many strict rules on labelling, a number of logos and claims that appear on foods fall under a 'voluntary labelling' category, meaning they are not subject to specific regulations.

This means that many claims about nutrition or health on a packet fall under these voluntary guidelines, so their legal meaning may not be clear.

Packaging is not just a way of informing the customer about what a product is and what it contains, but also needs to be recognised by parents as a marketing tool to sell more of a product. Food manufacturers are likely to draw your attention to the good points about a product on the front of the packaging but are unlikely to highlight the less virtuous details (which are more likely to be found somewhere on the back or not at all). Therefore, you need to inform yourselves to ensure you're making the choices you want to and not just being seduced into purchases.

THE CURRENT LEGISLATION ON CHILDREN'S FOODS

One of the reasons I decided to write this book was that I discovered there are no special regulations governing what can be present in foods aimed specifically at children (beyond infancy or those not subsisting on weaning foods). This includes specific children's ranges or those staple foods very commonly eaten by children, for example breakfast cereals, bread, confectionery and soft drinks.

There are detailed regulations for infant formulas and processed cereal-based foods for infants under twelve months, and regulations governing weaning foods for toddlers (The Processed Cereal-based Foods and Baby Foods for Infants and Young Children Regulations 2003, which came into force in March 2005). These regulations include strict limits on sugar, minimum contents of protein in meals, no added salt allowed, no sweeteners allowed, and no colourings, flavourings, preservatives or emulsifiers are to be added.

From the age of twelve months, and with any food not regarded as a weaning food, manufacturers adhere to the Food Labelling Regulations 1996. Therefore, just like standard adult foods, there are no actual limits on salt, sugar, fat or saturated fat, and any of the approved additives are permitted in these foods.

Given that children can be fussy consumers, adding sugar, food colourings, fat, flavourings and salt may help to make a product look more attractive and taste better for children's palates.

Considering the huge growth in foods specifically designed for (and marketed at) children I feel this means parents could be forgiven for making the assumption that special children's meal ranges, frozen chicken shapes, lunchbox marketed foods, yogurts and drinks with cartoon characters on, and other similar products are, if not 'good for', at least suitable for children. Unfortunately, this assumption cannot and should not be made and parents need to be able to arm themselves with the basic information contained in this book if they want to be able to make informed choices about what they feed to their children. Only then can they ensure their children are eating healthy and nutritious foods appropriate for their age.

Product Description

It is illegal for labels to have false information or misleading descriptions. This is true of a product name, any words or phrases used to describe the product on the front of the label, and also of any pictures on the label. A product cannot have a picture containing a particular food if that food is not present in the item in the form in which it is portrayed, as when a drink shows real fruit when it only has flavouring.

Ingredients List

Ingredients lists have to be written clearly and in order of descending weight. In other words, the first ingredient is the one that the product contains the most of. If any ingredient is mentioned in the product name, e.g. lamb hotpot, then that ingredient must be listed with the actual amount contained in the product as a percentage, e.g. 'Lamb (26%)'.

> **Ingredients:** Wholegrain wheat (65%), Sugar, Plain Chocolate (17%) (Sugar, Cocoa Mass, Cocoa Butter, Emulsifier: Soya lecithin), Salt, Flavourings.

Nutritional Information

It is not a legal requirement to give any information about the nutritional content of a product (e.g. calories, fat content) on the packaging if the manufacturer makes no claims about its nutritional content. This information is often supplied voluntarily by a manufacturer to inform the consumer.

Where any nutritional claims are made on a packet (e.g. 'reduced fat', 'high in fibre', 'low calorie') then the manufacturer is under a legal obligation to provide nutritional information. In this case the minimum amount of information a manufacturer need tell us about their product is:

	TYPICAL VALUES PER 100G/100ML
Energy	kJ/ kcal
Protein	g
Carbohydrate	g
Fat	g

For definitions of energy, kcal and kj, protein, carbohydrate and fat, see Chapter 3: What Every Parent Should Know About Children's Nutrition.

Further in-depth information can be provided by manufacturers voluntarily or as a legal requirement if they make a claim on the packaging related to any of the following: saturated fat, sugar content, fibre and salt. These will look like this on the label:

	TYPICAL VALUES PER 100G/100ML
Energy	kJ/ kcal
Protein	g
Carbohydrate	g
Of which: sugar	g
Fat	g
Of which: saturates	g
Fibre	g
Sodium	g

For definitions of sugar, saturated fat, fibre and salt, plus the recommended daily amounts for children, see Chapter 3: What Every Parent Should Know About Children's Nutrition.

Sometimes, a further breakdown of the fat content of a product to include polyunsaturated and monounsaturated fats is also listed, either voluntarily or through a legal requirement if any nutritional claim about these nutrients is made. For more information about these see Chapter 3: What Every Parent Should Know About Children's Nutrition.

On some products that I analysed there was also information given about the vitamins and minerals present where a product supplies a 'significant' amount. Legally, a 'significant amount' is 15 per cent or more of the recommended daily allowance of that vitamin or mineral per 100g/100ml, or per portion if the package contains only one portion. These are listed under the individual vitamins and mineral names, with the amounts given in weight and often also listed as a percentage of the recommended daily allowance (RDA). For more information about RDAs see page 16.

NUTRITION INFORMATION		
Typical Values	Per 30g Serving with 125ml semi-skimmed milk	Per 100g As Sold
ENERGY	756kJ (179 kcal)	1651kJ (389 kcal)
PROTEIN	6.6g	7.2g
CARBOHYDRATE	30.9g	83.1g
of which sugars	15.6g	32.1g
FAT	3.1g	3.1g
of which saturates	1.8g	1g.4
FIBRE	0.7g	2.5g
SODIUM	0.08g	0.27g
SALT EQUIVALENT	0.2g	0.6g
VITAMINS & MINERALS	Per 30g Serving with 125ml semi-skimmed milk	Per 100g As Sold
THIAMIN	0.4mg (28% RDA)	1.2mg (85% RDA)
(Vitamin B1)		
FOLIC ACID	57ug (29% RDA)	170ug (85% RDA)
RDA = Recommended daily Amount		
This pack contains approximately 12 servings of 30g		

> **TIP**
>
> In my analysis I found that products highlighting their vita-
> min and mineral contents were not necessarily products
> that would be regarded as balanced or healthy – they may
> still be high in sugar or salt. So it is always worth checking
> the packaging more thoroughly before making assump-
> tions as to the actual nutritional benefit of a product.

> **TIP**
>
> To assess the nutritional content of a product or to make
> comparisons between more than one product, always
> look at the nutritional content per 100g/100ml rather
> than per product or per portion.

WHAT ARE GUIDELINE DAILY AMOUNTS, RECOM-
MENDED DAILY AMOUNTS AND TRAFFIC
LIGHT LABELLING?

These are some of the ways that manufacturers and supermarkets are trying to help consumers make sense of the nutritional
information of a product. If you are standing in the supermarket
aisle trying to decide between one of two or more products for
your family then these information guides are intended to help
us to make healthier choices, or at least more informed choices,
about the foods we choose.

Guideline Daily Amounts (GDA)

These have been developed by food manufacturers and retailers. They give consumers an idea of the amount an average

person should be consuming of each of the main nutrients and dietary elements such as calories, fat, saturated fat, carbohydrate, total sugars, fibre, salt/sodium a day.

The idea is not that a person needs to eat 100 per cent of the GDA for every nutrient every day, but that this reading can give an indication of the contribution a product may make to their overall diet. As every individual is different in terms of size and activity levels, then GDAs should not be used as targets but simply a guide.

GDAs were calculated on the predicted daily consumption of an average consumer eating a diet conforming to current government guidelines on dietary requirements. They are therefore seen as being based upon, and consistent with, the latest published scientific data on dietary requirements and recommendations, and have been developed in consultation with recognised nutrition experts.

Each serving (2 slices) contains

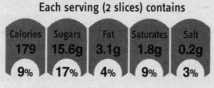

Calories	Sugars	Fat	Saturates	Salt
179	15.6g	3.1g	1.8g	0.2g
9%	17%	4%	9%	3%

of your guideline daily amount

How these are listed varies between product, manufacturer and retailer. Some list general Adult GDAs (which are actually the same as the readings for Women's GDAs) and others will list both the individual Men's and Women's GDAs.

For children in general the GDA most commonly used is that applicable to children aged from five to ten years. GDAs for girls and boys, as well as more specific ages, have been set but I did not find these listed on any of the 570 products I looked at. I have listed below what the current GDAs are for children.

CHILDREN AGED 5–10 YEARS (this is usually the one used on packaging)	
	5–10 years
Energy (Calories)	1,800
Protein (g)	24
Carbohydrates (g)	220
of which sugars (g)	85
Fat (g)	70
of which saturates (g)	20
Fibre (g)	15
Sodium (g)	1.1
Equivalent as salt (g)	3

Children by Gender (Ages 4–18 years)

GIRL'S GUIDELINE DAILY AMOUNTS				
	4–6 years	7–10 years	11–14 years	15–18 years
Energy (Calories)	1,550	1,750	1,850	2,100
Protein (g)	20	28	41	45
Carbohydrates (g)	195	220	230	265
of which sugars (g)	75	85	90	105
Fat (g)	60	70	70	80
of which saturates (g)	20	20	25	25
Fibre (g)	12	16	20	24
Sodium (g)	1.1	1.8	2.4	2.4
Equivalent as salt (g)	3	5	6	6

Source: IGD

BOY'S GUIDELINE DAILY AMOUNTS			
	4–6 years	7–10 years	11–14 years	15–18 years
Energy (Calories)	1,700	1,950	2,200	2,750
Protein (g)	20	28	42	55
Carbohydrates (g)	215	245	275	345
of which sugars (g)	85	100	110	140
Fat (g)	75	75	85	105
of which saturates (g)	20	25	25	35
Fibre (g)	12	16	20	24
Sodium (g)	1.1	1.8	2.4	2.4
Equivalent as salt (g)	3	5	6	6

There are no Guideline Daily Amounts for children under four years.

Whether a manufacturer or retailer chooses to list GDAs on their packaging is totally voluntary, not a legal requirement, so this information is not found on all products. However, more and more manufacturers and retailers are choosing to display this information.

A drawback I found when analysing the products aimed at children or those staple products (such as breakfast cereals) that are eaten commonly by children as well as adults is that there is often only a GDA listing for adults, which makes it hard for parents to gauge the product's nutritional value for their child's diet. Also, with small packs often involved, it is clearly difficult for manufacturers to fit this information on.

My Findings On GDAs

I found adult GDA information on approximately 30 per cent and child GDAs listed on approximately 10 per cent of the products I looked at.

Recommended Daily Amount (RDA)

The European Union has set Recommended Daily Amounts for vitamins and minerals. RDAs tend to appear most commonly within the nutritional information panel when the readings for specific vitamins and minerals are given. RDAs are estimates of the amounts of vitamins and minerals sufficient to meet, or more than meet, the optimal needs of adults.

For a food or drink to be allowed to mention that it contains a particular vitamin or mineral on its label, it must supply at least 15 per cent of the RDA for this vitamin or mineral per 100g or per 100ml (or per portion if only one portion is contained in a packet).

In the UK, estimated requirements for particular groups of the population are based on advice that was given by the Committee on Medical Aspects of Food and Nutrition Policy (COMA) back in the early 1990s. COMA examined the available scientific evidence and estimated nutritional requirements of various groups within the UK population. These were published in the 1991 report *Dietary Reference Values for Food Energy and Nutrients for the United Kingdom*. The Dietary Reference Values (DRVs) and the Reference Nutrient Intakes (RNIs) that are included within these readings are the basis for RDAs.

For a list of the RDAs for children for the commonly found nutrients on food packaging see page 16.

> **Note**
> Most labels that contain information about RDAs are based on adult requirements not those of children. However, on some of the specific children's ranges, RDAs for children are given.

Nutrients commonly found with RDAs on Nutritional Information panels

Taken from *UK Reference Nutrient Intakes* (compiled by COMA), 1991, children aged 1–18 years

Age	Vitamin B$_1$ (Thiamin) mg	Vitamin B$_2$ (Riboflavin) mg	Vitamin B$_3$ (Niacin) mg	Vitamin B$_6$ mg	Vitamin B$_{12}$ µg	Folate µg	Vitamin C mg
1–3	0.5	0.6	8	0.7	0.5	70	30
4–6	0.7	0.8	11	0.9	0.8	100	30
7–10	0.7	1.0	12	1.0	1.0	150	30
Males							
11–14	0.9	1.2	15	1.2	1.2	200	35
15–18	1.1	1.3	18	1.5	1.5	200	40
Females							
11–14	0.7	1.1	12	1.0	1.2	200	35

Age	Vitamin A µg	Vitamin D µg	Calcium mg	Magnesium mg	Potassium mg	Iron mg**	Zinc mg
1–3	400	7	350	85	800	6.9	5.0
4–6	500	*	450	120	1,100	6.1	6.5
7–10	500	*	550	200	2,000	8.7	7.0
Males		*					
11–14	600	*	1,000	280	3,100	11.3	9.0
15–18	700	*	1,000	300	3,500	11.3	9.5
Females		*					
11–14	600	*	800	280	3,100	14.8	9.0

* No recommended dietary intakes are given for children over 3 years. This is because the main source of Vitamin D is the action of sunlight on the skin. All children over this age who lead a normal lifestyle will meet their needs of this nutrient from exposure to sunlight.

** Iron requirements are greater in very young children aged 1–3 years than children aged 4–6.

Traffic Light Labelling

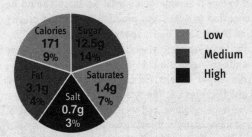

Traffic Light labelling lets you see at a glance whether a product you are thinking of buying has a high (red), medium (orange) or low (green) amount of particular nutrients such as fat, saturated fat, sugar, salt or calories. In a healthy diet we should all be aiming to eat less of these specific nutrients. The more green lights then the healthier the choice of product, and the more red lights the less healthy a product is.

Traffic Light labelling, though very simple to understand, is not without some drawbacks. For example, foods that are high in fruit may be given a red light for sugar and foods rich in healthy fats, such as salmon, may also be given a red light for fat under this system. However, both of these products are beneficial in a healthy diet.

Another drawback is found when making product comparisons. The Traffic Light system is often based on a serving size rather than 100g of a product, so this can make it harder to compare two or more products. For example, one loaf of bread may have a green light for salt per serving and another may have a red light per serving. When the serving size is looked at, two slices of the 'green' loaf may be much smaller in amount than two slices of the 'red' loaf.

The Food Standards Agency (FSA) has put together guidelines for manufacturers and retailers to follow so that even though Traffic Light labels may look different on different products they all follow the same guidelines. So there should be no trouble choosing between two products even if the precise representation of the traffic lights appears different.

The Traffic Light labelling system is supported not only by the Food Standards Agency but by many other health, medical and nutrition organisations, for example the British Medical Association and Diabetes UK. The system is also supported by a number of the large retailers and well-known manufacturers, with more and more manufacturers now adopting it. Consumer research carried out for the FSA seems to show that this is one of the easiest forms of labelling to understand, easier than the GDA system, for instance.

In January 2008 the Food Standards Agency commissioned a research company, in association with a UK university, to conduct a study to assess the impact that front-of-pack nutritional labelling is having on people's food choices.

My Findings on Traffic Light Labelling

I found Traffic Light labelling on less than 10 per cent of the products I looked at. On products such as bread and breakfast cereals, which children may be eating daily, I found that only adult readings are given, so the system offers no help to parents. Therefore, parents need to remember that when a product has a red light for salt or sugar, this is based on an adult body size and so is even more significant in the contribution of that nutrient when used as part of a child's diet.

WHAT ARE ADDITIVES?

The term 'additive' is used to describe any substance not normally eaten as a food in itself but which has been added to food to perform a particular function. Additives can play many roles, including helping to preserve food, increase its shelf life, keep it safe for consumption, help it to rise, to thicken it or just to make it look nicer.

Most food additives must be included either by name or by an E number in the ingredients list. The ingredients list should also tell you what role an additive plays. Additives are grouped in terms of their job functions, which include: preservatives, anti-oxidants, colours, emulsifiers, stabilisers, and gelling agents. The roles additives play in food are all listed in Appendix 1.

There are over 500 additives that are legally allowed to be added to our food. In addition to this there are more than 2,500 flavourings permitted for use in foods that do *not* need to be specified by name on a label. For more information on Flavourings see page 23.

WHAT ARE E NUMBERS: ARE THEY ALL BAD?

E numbers are very simply a numerical code for any additive used in foods. The 'E' prefix means that an additive has been approved for use in the European Union, i.e. that it has passed safety tests and has been deemed safe for use in foods. This approval is constantly being monitored, reviewed and amended in the light of new, ongoing scientific data.

E numbers/additives can be totally natural, totally synthetic (i.e. man-made) or synthetically made to mimic a natural substance.

Most additives are neutral. They play a role in food safety, food aesthetics and flavour or help increase shelf life but do not have any proven effect on the body, either beneficial or harmful, in the small amounts that are present in foods. Research seems to be highlighting some additives that may actually have beneficial roles in our health, for example Vitamin E (which is used as an antioxidant and preservative) and Lycopene (the red colour in tomatoes, which is used as a natural food colouring).

Some synthetically made and some natural additives have been linked over the years to adverse reactions in sensitive individuals, including asthma, behavioural problems, skin reactions and gastrointestinal upsets. In my research for this book I have found that reliable scientifically based data on additives and adverse reactions can be hard to find. There is much anecdotal evidence (i.e. reported effects) but few hard scientific facts. Parents should feel fairly at ease knowing that if there were hard scientific data on an additive causing an adverse reaction then this would be reviewed by the European Food Safety Agency (EFSA). If the evidence was found to be sufficiently proven then an additive would have its E number removed and be banned from use in foods.

However, I do feel that many parents would like to know whether there is any current scientific evidence to support claims that a particular adverse reaction may be triggered or made worse by an additive where these claims exist. This will particularly be the case if you have a child who suffers from any adverse reactions and allergies. I have noted this information in the A–Z Reference Guide so that you as a parent can make your own decision whether to control particular additives in your child's diet. This information does not mean these additives are not safe for the majority of children, but lets you make the right decisions for your own child about whether you want to exclude certain additives from their diets.

The A–Z Reference Guide can help you to decipher all the ingredients and additives found on ingredients lists. This provides you with a simple explanation and, where relevant, any further information I have found of a nutritional nature or a link to possible adverse reactions.

NUTRITION AND HEALTH CLAIMS: CAN THEY BE BELIEVED?

What Is a Nutrition Claim?

Legally, this is any statement that suggests a food or drink has a particular beneficial nutritional property due to the nutrients it contains or does not contain. Examples are 'low in fat', 'high in fibre' and 'no added sugar'.

What Is a Health Claim?

Legally, this is any statement about the beneficial effect on the body of a food or its ingredients, for example, 'helps maintain a healthy heart', 'helps maintain bone health' or 'helps aid digestion'.

To help protect consumers from misleading claims, new European legislation came into force in July 2007. Now any claims made in relation to the nutrition and health benefits of a food can only be made if the claims are based on science. This means a manufacturer or retailer has to be able to scientifically prove a claim. Some claims are not allowed to be used on the packaging of foods and drinks, such as those claiming that food can treat, prevent or cure any disease or medical condition.

Do Health and Nutrition Claims Mean a Product Is Good for My Child?

Specific health and nutrition claims that I found on some of the products I looked at are explained in depth in Chapter 5: Manufacturers' Claims: What Do They Really Mean?

Overall, the claim is usually made in relation to one specific nutrient in the product, and just because a product is low in fat or high in Vitamin C does not mean that it is also low in sugar or salt. Therefore, it is always best to check the nutritional information or ingredients list before making a final assessment about a product's suitability for your child.

The Tick Lists

> ✔ No added sugar
> ✔ No artificial preservatives or colours
> ✔ No hydrogenated fats
> ✔ No preservatives
> ✔ Good source of fibre
> ✔ Great for lunchboxes

These are becoming more and more common, especially on the packaging of products aimed at children. This seems to be the most common way that manufacturers are highlighting the good points of their products to parents.

The good news is that regulations mean these claims have to be truthful, cannot be misleading, and must be based on scientific facts. Many such as 'good source of fibre' or 'low in sugar' have to meet strict guidelines to be able to make these claims. For example, to be classed as high fibre, a product must contain at least 6g of fibre per 100g of product. For a product to be able to carry a nutrition or health claim it must have a healthy overall nutrient profile, so for a product to be allowed to claim it contains Vitamin C it must not contain too much fat, sugar or salt. The specific criteria for this, though, has not been decided upon and is currently being reviewed by the European Food Safety Authority (EFSA). It is due to be published in 2009.

For more information about these guidelines and claims see Chapter 5: Manufacturers' Claims: What Do They Really Mean?

My Findings

I found that though the tick boxes can provide important 'at a glance' information about a product, it must be kept in mind that the packaging is not only a source of information for the parent but is also an advert for the product written by the manufacturer. Just because the claims will not be untrue they do not automatically mean you can trust the product as a really healthy one for your child. For example, a product may be one that contains no artificial preservatives or flavours but may have a host of colours added to it, or it may have 'no added sugar' but this does not mean it doesn't contain other types of sugars, such as artificial sweeteners or naturally occurring fruit sugars.

For more information about specific claims see Chapter 5: Manufacturers' Claims: What Do They Really Mean?

Fresh, Pure and Natural

There is increasing pressure on manufacturers and retailers for more natural products, so the terms 'natural', 'pure' and 'fresh' are being used increasingly by manufacturers (and looked for by consumers) on packaging when making food and beverage choices.

In 2002 the Food Standards Agency (FSA) issued guidelines/recommendations for the food industry on how and when these terms should be used.

FLAVOURINGS

Flavourings are added to a wide range of foods but, being controlled by different laws to other food additives, they do not have E numbers.

A manufacturer has to list if flavourings have been used in

a product on the ingredients list but does not have to give their specific names. Usually just the term 'flavourings' is listed in the ingredients list. The word 'flavouring' covers any of more than 2,500 flavourings that are permitted for use in foods and drinks.

My Findings

Flavourings were listed on the ingredients list of 232 out of the 570 products I looked at, i.e. 40 per cent of the products. In a few of the product ranges I looked at nearly every product contained added flavourings.

The term 'natural flavourings' can only be used when the flavouring is extracted from plant or animal material. Where the term 'natural' is not used then it is likely that the flavourings are synthetic.

I found that in most of the products flavourings was either the last or nearly the last ingredient listed on the ingredients lists, which means that clearly only very small quantities are used in any one product.

If you are keen to minimise your child's intake of additives, including flavourings, then careful reading of labels will be required and, where possible, reducing their reliance on processed foods may be necessary.

COLOURINGS

These are sometimes used to replace the natural colour of a food that may have been lost during processing or storage, or to make products a consistent colour. Colours can make foods look more attractive to some people and this may be especially true for children. There are three types of colours that have E numbers and are thus approved for use in food and beverages in the EU:

1. Artificial food colours, which include some azo dyes; these were originally processed from coal tar but these days are made synthetically.
2. Inorganic pigments, made from metals like silver.
3. Natural colours that are obtained from natural plant and vegetable sources or are synthetically made to mimic these natural substances.

There is some uncertainty among scientists about whether azo dyes are linked to triggering conditions such as asthma and skin reactions or whether they are linked to hyperactivity. Research on such dyes has been carried out since the 1970s but evidence has not necessarily been conclusive. A recent study carried out by Southampton University (with funding help from the FSA) was published in the *Lancet* in 2007: 'Food additives and hyperactive behaviour in 3-year-old and 8/9-year-old children in the community: a randomised, double-blinded, placebo-controlled trial' (2007; 370: 1560–67). This study seems to indicate a link between certain combinations of particular artificial food colours, a preservative and an adverse effect on children's behaviour. The colours included in the study (all of which are azo dyes) are: sunset yellow (E110), quinoline yellow (E104), carmoisine (E122), allura red (E129), tartrazine (E102) and ponceau 4R (E124).

The FSA decided not to ban the additives but has asked the European Food Safety Authority to examine the research and make an EU-wide decision on their safety. This review is due out some time in 2008.

The FSA advice as of September 2007 is that it may be best to avoid these artificial food colours if your child shows signs of hyperactivity or Attention Deficit Hyperactivity Disorder (ADHD) as this may help improve their behaviour.

Many health campaigners think that artificial colourings should be removed from all foods and drinks, regarding them as unnecessary and potentially dangerous.

Some of these azo dyes are used in many children's medicines. Current EU guidelines mean that medicines have to carry a warning that artificial colourings 'may cause allergic reactions'. Foods and drinks carry no such warning, despite being consumed in much greater quantities.

My Findings

Of the 570 products I looked at 156 contained added food colourings, and of these 141 contained natural food colourings and 25 products contained azo dyes. Some of the products I looked at that contained azo dyes were cake mixes, confectionery, sweets, soft drinks and children's medicines (many of which state 'suitable from 2 or 3 months old').

If your child may be sensitive to what they eat then you will find further information about adverse reactions and food additives in Chapter 4: Adverse Reactions to Food.

Check packets carefully as ingredients do change, and more and more manufacturers are opting to use natural colours. There may also be changes in the law during 2008 with regards to the use of azo dyes. Check out the website – www.whatsinthis.co.uk – to keep up to date.

PRESERVATIVES

These are substances added to foods to ensure that a food remains safe to consume whilst on the shelf or in the supermarket chiller cabinet and, subsequently, your fridge or store cupboard. As a group they act in many different ways, from stopping or inhibiting harmful mould or the growth of bacteria, to the prevention of food discolouration or prolonging the shelf life of a product. In the old days the traditional way of preserving food was to use salt, vinegar or sugar. These are still used but there are also an ever-increasing number of other methods and substances being developed by constantly advancing technology. This is sometimes particularly necessary where new products are being developed such as low-sugar variants, where there is a need to replace the sugar (which acts as a natural preservative) with another preservative.

There are many natural preservatives used by the food industry as well as synthetically made ones.

Some groups of preservatives, for example sulphites, benzoates, nitrites and nitrates, have been linked to adverse reactions in children and adults such as asthma, skin reactions and behavioural problems. However, as with food colours, these links have not often been scientifically proven. The effect of consuming a mix of certain preservatives and colours in the same food or drink has also not been well researched.

The recent study carried out by Southampton University (published in 2007 in the *Lancet*) mentioned above under 'Colourings' also seems to indicate a link between certain combinations of artificial food colours and the preservative sodium benzoate (E211) and a negative effect on children's behaviour. EFSA is currently reviewing this study but in the meantime the Food Standards Agency advice as of September 2007 is that it may be best to avoid sodium benzoate (E211) if your child shows signs of hyperactivity or Attention Deficit Hyperactivity Disorder (ADHD) as this may help improve their behaviour.

Under EU guidelines, medicines should carry a warning that sodium benzoate may be 'mildly irritant to the skin, eyes and mucous membranes'. Foods and drinks carry no such warning, again, despite being consumed in much greater quantities.

Benzoates

The FSA advises that benzoic acid (E210) and other benzoates (E211, E212, E213, E214, E215, E216, E217, E218 and E219), which are all used as food preservatives to prevent yeasts and moulds from growing, could make the symptoms of asthma and eczema worse in children who already have these conditions. These are used in products such as soft drinks and children's medicines.

Sulphites

Sulphur dioxide (E220) and other sulphites (E221, E222, E223, E224, E226, E227 and E228) are all used as preservatives in foods and drinks. They are used in products such as soft drinks, dried fruit and processed meats such as sausages and burgers.

The FSA's advice on sulphites is that anyone who has asthma may react to inhaling sulphur dioxide and a few may react after consuming it.

Contains sulphites

Food-labelling regulations mean that a manufacturer is legally required to clearly state on the packet if a food or drink or an ingredient contained in the product contains sulphur dioxide or sulphites at levels above 10mg per kilogram or per litre.

My Findings

Of the 570 foods I looked at 80 (14 per cent) contained preservatives. With regard to benzoates these were found in nine of the products and sodium benzoate (E211) in six products. These were children's medicines, soft drinks, cheese products, meat products, savoury lunchbox products and one ready-meal. If your child may be sensitive to sodium benzoate or other benzoates then check labels carefully. I found sulphites in seventeen products, including fresh filled pasta, cordials and soft drinks, crisps, meat products and one cake product.

There has been a huge increase in dried fruit and dried-fruit bars aimed at children, so if your child may be sensitive to sulphur dioxide (E220) you will need to check the labels of these products carefully.

If your child is sensitive to food additives then you will find further information in Chapter 4: Adverse Reactions to Food.

SWEETENERS

There are currently fifteen sweeteners that have been approved for use in food and drinks and been assigned E numbers. These fall into two groups: bulk sweeteners and intense sweeteners.

Bulk Sweeteners

These are less sweet than sugar or are digested very slowly by the body, but are used in similar amounts to sugar. Examples are sorbitol (E420), maltitol (E965) and xylitol (E967).

Products using such sweeteners may not be significantly lower in calories than similar ones containing sugar, as these types of sweeteners contain calories. They are, however, friendlier to teeth than sugar.

Intense Sweeteners

These are many times sweeter than sugar so only very small amounts are used. Some are not digested by the body and pass straight through, which means they provide no calories. Others in this group do contain some calories, but because they are used in such tiny quantities they add very few calories to a product. Therefore, products containing them may be lower in calories than similar products made using table sugar. Examples are aspartame (E951), saccharin (E954), acesulfame-k (E950) and sucralose (E955).

Sweeteners may also be classified as natural (i.e. derived from carbohydrates found in nature) or artificial (i.e. produced synthetically and not present in nature).

Symptoms of dizziness, headaches and changes in mood have been attributed to aspartame but such claims have not been substantiated, despite much research being carried out over the last thirty or so years into its safety. The European Food Safety Authority has carried out a number of reviews on this research and currently feel there is no need to further review the evidence on the safety of aspartame. The last review was carried out in 2006.

As parents, of course, you may decide that you wish to limit your child's consumption of sweeteners. However, it must be remembered all sweeteners are non-cariogenic (i.e. they do not cause dental decay) as opposed to added sugar, which *is* cariogenic (so does cause tooth decay). Choosing to avoid the no-added-sugar, sugar-free or diet products which typically contain sweeteners may mean you need to be more careful that your child doesn't consume too much sugar, particularly in the form of soft drinks (e.g. cordials and fruit juices) and sweets.

Current Advice for Children Under Four Years Old
The current advice on sweeteners in children's diets is that if you give concentrated drinks that contain sweeteners to children under four, it is important to dilute them well.

For further advice on sugar intakes for your child see Chapter 3: What Every Parent Should Know About Children's Nutrition.

My Findings
Of the 570 products I looked at 28 contained sweeteners. All seven of the children's medicines I looked at contained sweeteners. The other products where I found sweeteners were some sugar-free varieties of drinks, sweets, puddings and baked beans.

BEST BEFORE / USE BY
Both these terms indicate how long a product will stay fresh and be safe to eat.

Best Before
This is a date after which the product may not be at its best, i.e. lose its flavour or texture, rather than a date after which a product is unsafe to consume. 'Best before' is found on products in tins, frozen foods, packets and dried foods; in other words, foods that tend to keep for longer.

Use By
This is a date after which the food may become unsafe to eat, i.e. it may make you ill. This tends to be found on fresh items that need to be eaten quite quickly such as meats, fish, dairy products and ready-meals.

ALLERGY INFORMATION
From November 2005, for pre-packaged foods, manufacturers and retailers have, by law, to state whether there are any of the following twelve ingredients in them, since they are all ones to which certain people may be allergic or intolerant. These are:
- Celery
- Cereals containing gluten (wheat, rye, oats, barley)
- Crustaceans
- Eggs
- Fish
- Milk
- Mustard
- Nuts such as almonds, hazelnuts, walnuts, Brazil nuts, pistachios and macadamia nuts
- Peanuts
- Sesame seeds
- Soya beans
- Sulphur dioxide and sulphites (see 'Preservatives') at levels above 10mg per kilogram or litre

Some food labels say 'may contain nuts', which means that though nuts might not have been used in the ingredients of a product, the product may have come into contact with a production or storage environment in which nuts are used. Therefore, if your child is allergic to nuts you will also need to avoid these products to be absolutely safe.

Some of the above ingredients won't be listed if they are

deemed to have been so highly processed that they are no longer able to cause allergic reactions, for example refined soya bean oil and glucose syrups made from wheat or barley. If this is the case then it does not need to be highlighted on the packaging.

SUITABLE FOR VEGETARIANS

A variety of vegetarian logos are used on packaging. At present there is no single legal definition in terms of 'vegetarian' and 'vegan' at either a UK or European level. This means that the 'Suitable for Vegetarians' logo is not currently regulated as to the exact requirements of a product in order for it to be labelled as such. However, it is a 'voluntary claim', meaning that when it is used on a packet it is illegal for the information to be false or misleading.

Products that carry the 'Vegetarian Society Approved' logo will have had to meet specific requirements set by the society to be allowed to use it. Similarly, products that carry the 'Vegan Society' logo will have had to meet specific requirements set by that society.

GLUTEN FREE

Claims about gluten are very important for people who have coeliac disease. Gluten is a binding protein found in the following grains: wheat, oats, rye and barley. For people diagnosed with coeliac disease, gluten can be harmful for their bodies, but the majority of the population do not have any problem digesting gluten.

The Department of Health recommends gluten should not be given to infants under six months old and this is why weaning foods and milk powders, and drinks suitable for this age group, are always labelled with gluten information.

If you need more information about coeliac disease and gluten then visit the Coeliac UK website at www.coeliac.co.uk.

PRODUCE ORIGIN

Some foods such as beef and certain fruit and vegetables have a legal requirement to state what country they have come from.

For most foods the country of origin does not need to be on the packaging.

Work is being done by the Food Standards Agency to change European rules on food labelling so that the 'country of origin' must be given on a wider range of foods, and clearer rules set out for use of the term 'produce of'. Some manufacturers and retailers are now voluntarily stating the place of origin in response to a growing number of consumers wishing to buy local produce or know where a product has come from.

LOGOS / ENDORSEMENTS / FOOD ASSURANCE SCHEMES

You will see a number of small symbols, logos and endorsements used on packaging. For example, you may have noticed a Lion Mark on eggs, a little red tractor on meat, or logos from organisations and charity health symbols such as the Health Education Trust, a tooth white logo from the British Dental Health Foundation, the 'Freedom Foods' (an RSPCA scheme) logo or the Diabetes UK logo.

Assurance Schemes

Examples of assurance schemes are the Lion Mark on eggs and the Red Tractor on meat. These both mean that the product has met basic standards in the way food has been grown and produced. Marks such as the Freedom Foods logo mean that slightly higher production standards have had to be met for these foods.

Most of these schemes are voluntary but the logos involved can only be used if independent inspections have certified that a product meets particular production standards for that food or industry. This means that not all manufacturers choose to use them. Also, the exact standards required to use a logo are not widely known to the consumer.

The Food Standards Agency is currently reviewing the assurance schemes and it may be that we will see more schemes becoming non-voluntary, with information about the exact standards that have to be met becoming more well known amongst the public.

The only assurance scheme that is not voluntary is the one for organic food. For more information see page 36: What Does Organic Mean?

Logos and Endorsements

Some of these are a little misleading as they may involve a manufacturer applying to use a logo of an organisation, undergoing an inspection and checks by this organisation and then paying the organisation to use their logo. These logos and endorsements can be a source of revenue for the organisation, many of whom are charitable ones, which can obviously be very positive for ongoing research funded by and support offered by these organisations. However, it must be remembered that any such logos and endorsements are awarded solely by these organisations, and not because an EU-wide set of regulations and standards has been met.

> **My Findings on the Marketing of Products Using Popular Characters**
>
> The use of popular children's characters is one way that manufacturers and retailers try to encourage 'pester power' from children towards parents as a way of selling more of a particular product. I found such characters on more than 35 per cent of the products I looked at.

VALUE/ECONOMY

The terms 'value' and 'economy' are used on packaging, particularly with supermarkets' own brands. There is currently no legal definition of these terms and they may be seen as indicating a product is of high quality but low price or that a product is of a standard quality at a basic price.

You usually have to look at individual ingredients lists to gain a clear picture of a product's nutrition provision.

For more information on supermarket own brands see Chapter 7: My Findings.

WHAT DOES ORGANIC MEAN?

Sales of organic food have rocketed in the last decade for a mixture of health and environmental reasons. More and more parents are choosing organic foods for their children.

To use the term 'organic' means that a food has been produced to standards that have been set by European laws. This covers things such as farming methods, the use of pesticides and artificial fertilisers, and controls the use of food additives in the final organic products.

The Department for Environment, Food and Rural Affairs (DEFRA) is the UK control body for organic foods. There are a number of organic certification bodies within the UK, for example The Soil Association, Organic Farmers and Growers, and

The Organic Food Federation, all of whom have to be registered by DEFRA and given a code number (e.g. UK4, UK 1). All food growers and producers wishing to use the label 'organic' must be registered with and approved by one of these certification bodies. All labels using the term 'organic' must also indicate the certification body, either by name or by code number.

It is not always possible to make a product from entirely organic ingredients, since not all ingredients are available in organic form. Manufacturers of organic foods are permitted to use specific non-organic ingredients provided that these make up no more than 5 per cent of the product. Examples of these ingredients include salt, certain permitted food additives, processing aids (e.g. raising agents), water and micro-organisms (e.g. yeast and vitamins and minerals).

Products that contain only between 70 and 95 per cent organic ingredients cannot use the label 'organic' on their packaging but can specify which ingredients are organic in the ingredients list. Products that contain less than 70 per cent organic ingredients cannot be certified or labelled as organic or containing organic ingredients.

What Are Some of the Main Rules for Organic Foods?

- Organic foods are not able to use any artificial food colourings. Three natural food colourings are permitted but the exact conditions in which they can be used are also specified. See a full list of permitted additives in organic foods in Appendix 2.
- No artificial flavourings are allowed.
- The preservative sulphur dioxide (E220) is allowed only for use in wine and cider and not foods.
- Organic foods have minimum pesticide and artificial-fertiliser residues and veterinary-medicines residues.
- Hydrogenated fat is not allowed. For more information on

hydrogenated fat see Chapter 3: What Every Parent Should Know About Children's Nutrition.
- No flavour enhancers are allowed.
- No sweeteners are allowed.
- No genetically modified (GM) ingredients are allowed.

A still-contentious issue is whether organic foods naturally contain more nutrients – such as vitamins and minerals and essential fats – than non-organic foods. Some studies seem to indicate this may be the case with specific nutrients but more research is still needed.

What Does Organic *Not* Mean?
- Although organic foods are lower in pesticide residues, which may be beneficial for our health, the term 'organic' does not mean a product is automatically 'healthy'. You could have an organic product that is high in saturated fat or high in salt or sugar. It is still important to look at the ingredients lists and any nutritional information provided on organic products when buying for your child.
- Organic does not mean additive-free. There are currently 47 additives permitted in organic food. These are reviewed regularly in light of new information and research, and the most recent review was carried out towards the end of 2007. A full list of the permitted additives is given in Appendix 2. Please note that this list represents the minimum standards set by EU regulations and individual certification bodies may set stricter standards (i.e. choose not to permit some of these additives in products certified by themselves).

> ### My Findings
> Of the 570 products I looked at 47 were certified organic.

WHAT ARE GENETICALLY MODIFIED FOODS?

Genetic modification is a relatively new process and has many potential applications for the food industry.

Genetic modification is when foods are modified (changed or altered) by genetic techniques to confer new properties such as enhanced nutritional values, extended shelf life or greater resistance to disease, insects or fungi.

Genetic techniques are in vitro (i.e. in a laboratory) manipulations of genetic material, i.e. the genes. Genes contain all the growing and development functions for a plant or animal, including the DNA.

Current Legislation

Any GM foods intended for sale in the European Union are subject to a rigorous safety assessment, which is the responsibility of the European Food Safety Authority (EFSA). The Food Standards Agency is the UK authority named in the European legislation. The FSA is advised by an independent body of experts on the safety of GM foods. In June 2000 the FSA said that it was satisfied that the safety-assessment procedures for GM foods were sufficiently robust and rigorous to ensure that approved GM foods were as safe as their non-GM counterparts, and posed no additional risk to the consumer.

Manufacturers are required by law to indicate on the packaging when a product contains more than 0.9 per cent of a genetically modified ingredient, and all genetically modified ingredients must be mentioned with the words 'genetically modified' in the ingredients list.

Many people are yet to be convinced of the safety of GM foods and have concerns over the long-term health effects of consuming these foods. However, very little scientific data currently exists to support these fears.

> **My Findings**
> Out of the 570 products I looked at none were labelled as containing genetically modified ingredients.

WHAT DOES FAIRTRADE MEAN?

The Fairtrade mark is a sign that a product has met international Fairtrade standards, which have been set by the international certification body, the Fairtrade Labelling Organisations International (FLO). The Fairtrade mark is a guarantee that disadvantaged producers in the Third World are getting a better deal – they receive a minimum price, which covers the cost of sustainable production, and then also receive an extra premium that is invested in social or economic development projects.

WHAT DOES GLYCAEMIC INDEX MEAN?

Glycaemic Index (GI) has become a familiar term over the last few years but many people are still not sure exactly what it means or how they could use some knowledge of it to make healthier choices for themselves and their families.

GI is a ranking system for carbohydrate-containing foods based on their effect on blood-sugar (glucose) levels. For more information about carbohydrates see Chapter 3: What Every Parent Should Know About Children's Nutrition.

The GI scale runs from 0 to 100 and usually uses glucose (which has a GI value of 100) as a reference point. The effect other foods have on blood-sugar levels are then compared to this.

High GI food is defined as when a food is quickly digested and absorbed by the body, and it tends to cause a quick rise in blood-sugar levels. GI values of 70 or more are considered high.

Low GI food is when a food is digested and absorbed slowly by the body and does not tend to cause sharp rises in blood-sugar levels. GI values of 55 or less are considered low.

Does GI Have a Scientific Basis?

There is good scientific evidence that GI influences blood-glucose levels and it is used in the treatment of diabetes. Slow, steady rises and falls in glucose may help to keep you feeling full for longer. Low GI foods may help in weight management for both children and adults because they are absorbed more slowly from the GI tract into the bloodstream, which leads to feeling fuller for a longer period of time.

Why Is GI of Interest to Parents?

- Blood sugar is the body's main source of energy and fuels all the cells in the body including your brain and muscles. High surges of blood sugar can lead to blood sugar being released to the body's cells very quickly causing blood sugar to fall quickly. Low blood-sugar levels mean that the brain and muscles may be affected. This may cause low energy levels, mood changes, behavioural changes and poor concentration in children. Therefore, keeping blood-sugar levels constant in children may help them to concentrate better and for longer, and improve their mood swings and behaviour as well as boosting their energy levels for work, play and sport.
- Weight management: High GI foods digest more quickly so children may tend to snack more and could end up consuming too many calories and putting on weight. By choosing plenty of low GI foods your child will digest their food more slowly and the energy will be released from them slowly over a number of hours.

It's Not Foolproof for Children . . .

- We rarely eat an individual food on its own and one food will affect the absorption rate and blood-sugar rise of another food when eaten together. For example, a child may eat a white-bread (high GI) sandwich filled with cheese and ham (low GI) or a jacket potato (higher GI) with baked beans (medium GI) – this means that the lower GI foods will slow down the digestion of the high GI foods so as to create a more medium or low GI-value meal.

- Foods with a high GI are not necessarily unhealthy for children to eat – some fruits have a high GI value. Conversely, some lower GI foods are not particularly 'healthy' ones to eat in quantity (e.g. chocolate).

- Carbohydrate-free foods such as meats and cheese have a zero GI rating but they are not necessarily foods that should be eaten in unlimited quantities, even by children, because of their high saturated fat content.

- Young children have a great need for energy during each day. Parents need to be careful of over-providing diets that are very rich in low GI foods as these can often be ones that don't provide many calories and, as a consequence, may not provide sufficient energy for a rapidly growing child.

- It is important to be aware of the GI system as a parent and use it to help control excessive surges in blood sugar in your children – but ensure you also include in their diet some calorie-dense (high-calorie) foods. As GI is not an indicator of calorie content, there are some calorie-dense foods which have lower GI values as well as some high GI foods which are also very calorie dense.

WHAT ARE FUNCTIONAL FOODS?

Functional foods are foods that have a health-promoting benefit over and above their basic nutritional value.

They include a wide range of products:
- Foods generated around a particular functional ingredient, for example plant sterols in some margarines, omega-3 oils added to certain breads.
- Foods naturally rich in particular nutrients, for example probiotics in certain yogurts.
- Staple everyday foods that have been fortified with a nutrient that would not otherwise be present to any great extent, for example fortified breakfast cereals, bread, flour.

Health claims on packaging about the beneficial effect of a food or an ingredient in a product are controlled by an EU regulation that came into force in December 2006. This has allowed some well-established claims to be made, and other claims are now undergoing further research to make sure they can be scientifically substantiated, whilst some claims have been prohibited.

Functional Foods for Children

The common functional foods in children's diets are probiotics, prebiotics, omega-3 oils and calcium. I found these in yogurts, yogurt drinks, breakfast cereals, ready-meals and cheese products.

Though there may be some benefit to a child's nutritional status or health from consuming some of these 'functional foods' others can be expensive and are not necessarily all-round healthy foods – for example, some of the functional foods I looked at also contained a lot of sugar.

Probiotics

These are good bacteria that are found in our gut and are thought to help maintain a healthy digestive system and may also strengthen our immune systems. These bacteria are found naturally in some food products (e.g. yogurts) and are also now added to food products. Much research has been carried out into whether adding large amounts of these bacteria into our diets can actually be beneficial for our bodies but, as yet, health professionals such as dieticians do not feel the evidence is sufficient to make specific recommendations.

Prebiotics

These are types of carbohydrates that only our gut bacteria can feed on. Eating more prebiotics therefore causes more good bacteria to grow in our stomachs. The main types of prebiotics are inulin and fructose-oligosaccharides (FOS). They occur naturally in some foods (e.g. onions, garlic, asparagus and bananas). Some manufacturers are adding prebiotics to foods.

There seems to be a growing body of scientific evidence on the health benefits of prebiotics, however, more research is required before the actual amounts needed are confirmed and so there is no current recommended dose for adults or children. Health professionals currently make no specific recommendation.

Omega-3 Oils

Omega-3 oils are a healthy type of fat for the body that are obtained from two main sources: oily fish (including salmon, fresh tuna, sardines, trout, mackerel) and some plants (including some cereals and seeds). Manufacturers are now starting to add omega-3 oils to a variety of products, including some aimed at children, for example breads, yogurts, soft drinks and spreads.

There has been much research into the health benefits of omega-3 oils in the diet and some pretty well-established health benefits are now linked to it. These include helping to protect against heart disease and being vital for the healthy development of a baby's brain and eyes during pregnancy and the first six to twelve months of life (they are found naturally in breast milk and are added to all infant formulas).

There has been some research into whether taking omega-3 supplements could help with concentration and learning difficulties such as dyslexia, autistic spectrum disorders (ASD) and behavioural difficulties. The research as yet has not been conclusive.

Consuming foods that have been enriched with omega-3 can be a way to get these into the diet of some children who dislike oily fish. However, always read nutrition labels and ingredients lists carefully, as not all of these products may be 'healthy' for children in large amounts (they may be high in sugar or salt).

For further recommendations on fat intake see Chapter 3: What Every Parent Should Know About Children's Nutrition.

Calcium

This is added to a number of foods specifically aimed at children and to some staple foods, for example breakfast cereals, breads and fruit juices, that are consumed regularly by children. Calcium is essential for the development of bones and healthy teeth in children.

Alongside foods that are natural sources of calcium, consuming foods enriched with calcium may be beneficial in boosting a child's calcium intake, especially where they are intolerant, allergic to or dislike milk and other dairy products. Again, always read nutrition labels and ingredients lists carefully as not all of these products may be 'healthy' for children in large amounts (they may be high in sugar or salt).

FRESH BAKERY ITEMS / FRESH DELI FOODS / FRESH FISH AND MEAT COUNTERS

Products which don't have packaging such as fresh bakery items, meat, fish and deli foods from the fresh counters are governed by different labelling regulations to pre-packaged foods.

With these foods any allergens have to be stated clearly next to the product, as well as if the product has been irradiated or contains any genetically modified ingredients. No nutritional information needs to be given and the ingredients list is not legally required to be displayed unless specific claims about the product have been made e.g. that the product is low in fat. For meat products the amount of meat a product contains has to be labelled e.g. contains 7% chicken. With regards to additives, the category of additive used in a product legally has to be displayed on information for the customer but not the specific additive i.e. they have to note that a product contains emulsifiers or flavour enhancers but not state the specific name or E number.

It is the retailers' responsibility to make sure they have all of this information from the manufacturers or producers, so if you are in any doubt, ask.

chapter 3

What Every Parent Should Know About Children's Nutrition

INTRODUCTION

It can be hard for parents, even those with some knowledge of nutrition, to assess whether a food is suitable or good for their child. This is because children have different nutritional requirements from adults, plus there is not always full nutritional information listed on the packaging and even less frequently is there information about the specific requirements of children listed.

The information below is a background to the nutritional information you may find on food packaging as well as a guide to help you if not enough information is on the packaging.

Under 5s

Another issue with children's nutrition is that the standard healthy eating guidelines set by the government in association with health professionals are not intended to apply in full to pre-school children (those aged from one to five years).
This is because:

- Children of this age are growing rapidly and are often very active so they have higher nutrient and energy requirements in proportion to their size than adults.
- Young children also have very small stomachs and this can make it difficult for them to get enough energy and nutrients into their bodies each day if they are following adult 'healthy eating' guidelines, which are often higher in fibre and can contain lots of low-calorie and low-fat foods. Such diets can also sometimes reduce the amount of certain

essential nutrients, such as iron and calcium, that their bodies can absorb.

However, as the early years are often a time when lifetime food preferences are established, it is very important that children of this age eat a wide variety of basically healthy foods. This is also important for dental health (even with the milk teeth), bone development, a healthy immune system and their ability to learn and play.

Over 5s

Current recommendations are that by the time a child is five years old they should be eating very much the foods the whole family are eating and have a diet that corresponds to standard 'healthy eating guidelines'. A healthy diet is important for children of this age because:

- Children over five are starting to make more of their own choices for foods and take some responsibility for their own food intake. This means it is very important that they understand the need for a healthy diet and see the whole family eating this way too.
- Children of this age are still growing rapidly so need sufficient energy and vitamins and minerals each day. This is more likely to be achieved by eating a wide variety of healthy foods and restricting 'treats' to a minimum.
- Children's bones are developing at this age so good nutrition is essential for strong bones.
- A wide variety of nutritious food is important for a strong immune system.
- Children of school age need to be able to concentrate for periods each day. This may be harder with diets that provide foods that digest very quickly and don't provide lasting energy.

- These days, some children of this age are fairly inactive, which means they may not have such a high need for energy. This should be reflected in their diet, keeping high-fat and high-sugar foods to a minimum. However, the Chief Medical Officer's recommendation (in 2004) is that children of this age have a minimum of sixty minutes a day of at least moderate-intensity exercise.
- The diet of children of this age needs to be teeth-friendly, especially as this is a time when milk teeth are replaced with adult teeth.

The information below will help you to make informed but quick and easy decisions about a product when shopping as well as when planning meals, snacks and drinks.

WHAT ARE CALORIES?
The energy a food provides our body with is measured in 'kilo-calories' which tends to be shortened to 'calories' or 'kcal'. Calories are simply a way of measuring energy in food.

How Are They Labelled on Packaging?
If a packet has a nutrition label then calories will be listed as follows:

	Per portion	Per 100g/100ml
Energy	kj	kj
	kcal	kcal

What Does 'kJ' Stand For?

This stands for kilojoule, which is just another way of measuring the energy a food provides.

Calories and Children

In proportion to their size, children, especially young children, have much greater needs for calories/energy from food than adults. This is because children's bodies are growing rapidly and they are usually much more active than adults.

Calories are very much affected by the type and range of nutrients there are present in a food – if a food is high in fat or sugar then it is likely that the calories will also be high. Therefore, to make it as simple and quick as possible for you when shopping or when looking at some of the foods in your cupboard, I suggest you focus specifically on the fat and sugar contents of a food.

WHAT ARE CARBOHYDRATES?

Carbohydrates are a type of food that supplies us with energy. All carbohydrate foods are broken down (digested) in our bodies into glucose, which provides us with blood sugar and is used by every cell in our bodies for energy.

How quickly a food is digested into glucose (blood sugar) is determined by the type of carbohydrate food we have consumed.

There are two different types of carbohydrate foods:

1. **Starches or complex carbohydrates**
   These are foods such as rice, bread, potatoes, flour, pasta, noodles, sweet potatoes, butternut squash, breakfast cereals, crumpets, muffins, buns and scones. These foods,

especially the wholegrain versions, digest more slowly than the sugary group and so provide a more lasting energy for the body. These foods are also typically a source of other important nutrients such as fibre and B-vitamins. Children should try to get most of their energy from these types of carbohydrates rather than from the sugars group.

2. **Sugars or simple carbohydrates**
These are foods such as table sugar (also known as sucrose), fructose (fruit sugar), glucose, honey or foods containing high amounts of these (e.g. sweets, full-sugar drinks, sweetened breakfast cereals and yogurts). Sugars digest quickly and break down into glucose quickly, causing a sharper rise in blood sugar. This means the energy provided from these types of foods is not a lasting form of energy and can actually lead to low blood sugar (i.e. low energy levels). Sugars are also seen as the main nutrient associated with dental caries (tooth decay).

Glycaemic Index (GI) values for carbohydrate foods can be helpful in determining which of the above two groups a particular carbohydrate-rich food belongs to. For more information about GI values see 'What Does Glycaemic Index Mean?' in Chapter 2.

White bread digests as quickly as some sugars – it has been so highly processed and the fibrous parts of the wheat grain removed, that it should be seen as providing the body with more sugar than starch.

How Will Carbohydrate Be Listed on a Food Label?

Sometimes a label will just list total carbohydrate content (which includes the starch and sugar content). Alternatively, the amount of the different types of carbohydrate may be listed. If the product mentions any nutritional or health claim about sugar then they legally have to give the breakdown of types of carbohydrates on the label.

Fruits contain natural fruit sugar, but in whole fruits it is incorporated into the cellular structure of the fruit, which is high in fibre. This means that whole fruits should not be treated as just simple sugar foods. In fruit juice, on the other hand, the fruit sugar is not incorporated with the fibrous part of the fruit so these are digested faster than whole fruits and should be treated as high in sugar.

Carbohydrates and Children

It is recommended that children consume some starchy carbohydrate with each meal. This will provide children with some of the essential energy their bodies need. These don't always have to be wholegrain varieties but it is important that these are eaten some of the time, as they will provide children with some of the other essential nutrients their bodies need.

IS SUGAR BAD FOR MY CHILD?

Sugar itself should not be seen as bad but most children eat too much of it and this is what causes health and dental problems. Added sugars also provide no nutrients for children's bodies, only calories. It is recommended that children's sugar intake should be limited and that products such as sugary foods, drinks and sweets be kept as 'occasional treats'.

What Does a High Sugar Intake Mean for My Child?

- Sugar is the key nutrient associated with dental decay.
- Sugary foods and drinks can contribute to children's weight problems if they result in children eating more calories than their body requires each day. This is always a danger as, being high in sugar, these foods combine an appealing taste with high calories.
- A high sugar intake can be associated with poor energy levels and poor concentration levels. This is because foods high in sugar will digest quickly to cause a sharp rise in blood-sugar levels. This sharp rise will encourage blood sugar to be released to the body's cells quickly leaving low blood-sugar levels. Low blood-sugar levels mean that the body's cells, including muscles and the brain, will not have the energy necessary to function optimally.
- Also, because of this effect on blood-sugar levels, a high sugar intake may also cause mild mood swings and behavioural problems.
- Sleep may also be affected as low blood-sugar levels during the night may affect the deepness of the sleep, and even cause wakefulness, since the body may wake in a bid to encourage food to be eaten in order to raise blood-sugar levels.

It can be more difficult than you think to keep children's intake of sugar low, as sugar is found in so many sweet and savoury processed foods. A child does not have to be eating large amounts of the obvious sugary foods and drinks such as sweets, chocolate, biscuits, frosted breakfast cereals, fizzy drinks, etc. to be still consuming large amounts of sugar. This can make it hard for parents to gauge how much sugar their child is eating. Adding to the problem, much packaging can also be pretty complicated, making it hard to easily assess when a product contains a lot of sugar.

What Products Is Sugar Found in?

Besides the obvious culprits such as sweets, fizzy drinks, cordials, chocolate, biscuits, cakes, cake mixes, jams, puddings and frosted or chocolate breakfast cereals, many other foods and drinks I analysed contained significant amounts of 'added' sugar, including ready-meals, frozen meat products, fruit juices and smoothies, healthier and wholegrain breakfast cereals, fruit and cereal snack bars, breads, sauces such as tomato ketchup, fresh and tinned soups, jars of sauces for pasta and Chinese dishes, baked beans and yogurts. Sugar is also found in some children's medicines to disguise the taste of the actual medicinal ingredients.

> With fat-reduced versions of foods, sugar is often added in greater quantities than in the standard versions of foods as a way of replacing the taste normally provided by fat.

How Much Sugar Should My Child Eat?

For children between five and ten years old, the recommended Guideline Daily Amount (GDA) is 85g of sugars.

The current recommendation from health professionals, such as dieticians and nutritionists, is that no more than 10 per cent of our calories should come from sugar.

The FSA guidelines are as follows:

- A product is regarded as **HIGH IN SUGAR** if it has more than 15g of sugar per 100g.
- A product is regarded as **MEDIUM/MODERATE IN SUGAR** if it has between 5 and 15g of sugar per 100g.

- A product is regarded as **LOW IN SUGAR** if it has less than 5g of sugar per 100g.

> Remember that fruit juices, fruit smoothies, dried-fruit bars, fruit and cereal bars and dried fruit may be seen as 'healthy' for children but these can often contain large amounts of sugar. This sugar is sometimes in the form of 'added sugar' (i.e. table sugar), or a sugar such as honey has been added to a product, or it can also be from the naturally found sugars in a product such as fruit sugar. It is always best to check the nutritional information or ingredients lists before making assumptions that such foods are invariably healthy.
>
> In fact, in my findings, I observed a number of these supposedly 'healthier' snacks and drinks actually containing more total sugar (from a mix of naturally present sugars and added sugars) than some of the classic 'unhealthy' versions (e.g. of fizzy drinks and confectionery). See Chapter 7: My Findings for more information on this.

How Can I Work Out How Much Sugar a Product Contains?

There are four ways to get an indication of how high in sugar a product is:

1. **Nutritional information on the packet**

   Sugars can be listed within the total carbohydrates or, ideally, they will listed under their own separate heading. An example of how a label may look is:

	Per portion	Per 100g/100ml
Carbohydrate	30g	50g
of which sugars	20g	25gl

If sugars are not listed separately then the best way to find out if the product contains a lot of sugar is by looking at the ingredients list (see point 3 below).

2. The Really Simple Test

One teaspoon equals approximately 5g, so using this knowledge it is possible to quickly add up how many teaspoons of sugar your child would consume (or does consume) eating a particular product. For example, a child's pot of sweetened fruit yogurt may contain 17g of sugars (found within the nutritional information table), therefore it contains approximately 3½ teaspoons of sugar. Does this sound like a lot to you? If you had the same amount of natural yogurt would you add that amount of sugar yourself to the yogurt or do you feel it would be too much? Ask yourself these questions and it's likely that your 'gut' instinct (no pun intended!) on the answers is correct.

3. The ingredients list

The ingredients list always mentions ingredients in descending order, i.e. the higher up a list an ingredient then the more of that ingredient there will be in the product. You may well find that there are four or five different sugars in a single product all listed separately.

If an ingredient ends with 'ose' you can be pretty certain it's a sugar, e.g. glucose, fructose, sucrose, maltose, dextrose.

There are also many other ingredients that constitute a way of adding sugar to a product and which you need to look out for, e.g. honey, glucose syrup, golden syrup, invert

sugar, molasses, maple syrup, corn syrup, lactose, hydro-
lysed starch, treacle, raw/brown or demerara sugar.

4. **Traffic Light labelling**
This may not appear on all packaging but when it does it
can be an easy way of telling whether a particular product
is high in sugar – sugar will be red. For more information
about Traffic Light labelling see Chapter 2: What Every Parent
Should Know About Food Labels.

Note that this data is often based on adult guideline
amounts. If it is, then you need bear this in mind when
choosing the product for your child.

How Can I Compare Products?

The best way to compare the sugar contents of two or more
products is by looking under the nutritional information and
comparing the amount of sugar per 100g.

Are Some Sugars More Unhealthy Than Others?

Is brown sugar healthier than white?

Brown sugar is a slightly less-processed sugar than white
sugar, so it may contain slightly higher levels of some minerals
compared to white sugar, but otherwise it is exactly the same.

Is fruit sugar better for my child than table sugar?

- Fresh fruit – when talking about fresh fruit then there is no
  contest. Fresh fruit contains other vitamins and minerals as
  well as some fibre. Sugar contains none of these. Fresh fruit
  is also not associated with dental caries. This also includes
  fresh, frozen and unsweetened tinned fruit.
- Fruit juice – this is usually quite high in sugar mainly
  because when fruits are juiced they lose their fibre content,

plus there can be up to four or five oranges in a 250ml glass of juice and most people would struggle to consume five fresh oranges in one sitting. Fruit juice is also potentially associated with dental caries and certainly can lead to dental erosion (from the fruit acid content rather than the sugar content).

- Dried fruit – though a source of fibre, dried fruit again is quite concentrated in sugar, thanks to the drying process. Furthermore, as with fruit juice, it is possible to easily consume quite a large handful of dried fruit in one sitting in comparison to fresh fruit. The other issue with dried fruit is that dentists regard the stickiness of dried fruit as similar to toffee on the teeth. However, the good fibre contents and high calorie contents may be useful for some children if they are struggling to get these nutrients sufficiently from the rest of their diet.

- Fructose – when fruit sugar (fructose) is listed as an independent ingredient in a product it should be seen as a simple sugar carbohydrate and not in any way healthier than other forms of sugar.

Conclusion
Whole fresh fruits are the healthiest option for children. Fruit juices and dried fruits have some place within children's diets as a source of some nutrients and fibre but do also have some negative points. Fructose, like added table sugars, provides the body with no nutrients other than calories and should be avoided where possible.

Should I Always Choose 'No Added Sugar' Products?
The term 'no added sugar' can mean three things:
1. That a product contains very little sugar in total.
2. That a product does not contain 'added' sugar but may still

contain significant amounts of natural fruit sugars and could still, therefore, be classed as high in sugar.
3. That a product may contain artificial sweeteners in replacement of the sugar.

Therefore, 'no added sugar' claims do not automatically make a product healthy or good for children. You will need to check the ingredients list and the nutritional information table to be certain which of the above is the case. Depending on what you would like your child to consume, you will then need to make a choice about that particular food.

WHAT IS PROTEIN?

Protein is a nutrient that the body needs in order to be able to grow and repair itself. Protein-rich foods are: meat, fish, milk and dairy products, eggs, beans and lentils (pulses), and nuts.

Why Is Protein So Important in Children's Diets?
• Children's bodies need protein to be able to grow properly.
• Protein is also necessary for a healthy immune system and chemical reactions within cells.
• Protein digests slowly and causes no sharp rises in blood sugar, therefore by adding some protein to each meal this can help to keep energy levels balanced. Examples are breakfast cereals and milk, beans on toast, pasta with a Bolognese sauce.
• Protein-rich foods are also a source of iron, which is important for children.
• Dairy products are an important source of calcium for children.

> **How Much Protein Does My Child Need?**
> The guideline daily amount for children five to ten years old is 24g.

ALL ABOUT FATS

How Much Fat Should My Child Eat?

Children under five years of age have a slightly higher requirement for calories in proportion to their size than older children and adults. This means they will need some foods that are higher in fat, like whole-fat milk and cheese.

An average child of five to ten years of age needs approximately 70g of fat per day.

Omega-3 oils, which come from oily fish and a few plant sources, are important fats to include in the diet. It is recommended children eat the following amounts weekly:

Over 12	Two portions of oily fish a week
7 to 11 years	Two thirds of a portion
4 to 6 years	Half a portion
18 months to 3 years	One third of a portion

Oily fish include fish such as salmon, mackerel, trout, sardines, pilchards or fresh tuna. A portion is about 140g cooked.

Other sources of these omega 3 oils include some seeds such as linseeds, whilst some brands of eggs, bread, milk and margarine are specifically enriched with omega 3 oils and can help contribute to a child's requirement for these oils.

Are All Fats Bad?

No, not all fat is bad. The impact fat has on our health is down to the amount we eat as well as the type of fat. There are three different types of fat to which you will find references on food packaging:

1. **Saturated Fat**

   This type of fat is found in all animal products (e.g. red meat) and high-fat dairy products such as milk, cheese, butter and cream. Any fats that are hard or solid at room temperature are saturated fats. Saturated fats are not regarded as very healthy if eaten in large amounts. This still holds true for children. However, some foods that contain saturated fats can be important for children as sources of protein, iron and calcium, like red meat, whole milk and cheese. It is recommended that children have only whole milk until they are at least two years of age. Other foods rich in saturated fat can be eaten but in moderation.

2. **Unsaturated Fat**

   These are healthier fats for the body and can usually be identified by the fact that they are liquid at room temperature. The terms polyunsaturated and monounsaturated fats covers all vegetable oils, nut oils and seed oils, for example sunflower oil, olive oil and also the omega-3 fish oils. The exceptions are palm oil and coconut oil (which are rich in saturated fats). Unsaturated fats should form part of a child's diet but also in moderation.

3. **Hydrogenated Fats and Trans Fats**

   Hydrogenation is a process that can turn a liquid fat at room temperature into a solid fat. This can help make a fat more stable to use in food processing and also to increase its shelf life. During this process trans fats may be formed, so any product containing hydrogenated fat may also contain trans fats. Trans fats have been linked to raising cholesterol levels in the body and some research even suggests that they are worse for our health than saturated fat. Hydrogenated and trans fats have no known nutritional benefit, and it is recommended that both children and adults limit foods containing these fats in their diet to a minimum. Hydrogenated fats have to be mentioned in the ingredients list if present in a product.

My Findings
I noticed that only 25 food products I looked at contained hydrogenated fat (these were all cakes, biscuits and puddings) and many products were labelled with the nutritional claim 'No hydrogenated fat'. This has been a voluntary change for the better by food manufacturers.

HOW MUCH SALT SHOULD MY CHILD EAT?
Salt is a mineral made up of two elements: sodium and chloride. It is the sodium part that has been linked to health issues such as raised blood pressure. This is why on food labels you will often see either just an amount listed under sodium, or a listing of both a food's sodium and salt content.

Salt is found naturally in many foods but it is the 'added salt' that needs to be labelled.

Where Will I Find Salt?
Unfortunately, salt is added in varying amounts to a huge number of both savoury and sweet foods. I found it in ready-meals, crisps, savoury snacks, lunchbox items, cooked meats and meat products, processed cheese products, drinks, tinned

food, food in jars, soups, baked beans, frozen meat and fish shapes, cakes, biscuits, breakfast cereals, bread, condiments, spreads and butter.

Therefore, it is an ingredient that every parent really needs to be quite vigilant about, as a child can easily consume more than the recommended amounts.

What Is a High and Low Salt Content per 100g of Food?

High is more than 1.5g salt per 100g (or 0.6g sodium)
Low is 0.3g salt or less per 100g (or 0.1g sodium)

Salt and Children

For infants and weaning foods the food regulations mean that no added salt can be put into foods, drinks and formula milks. This is because babies' kidneys are not able to deal with very much salt. You should avoid adding salt to any foods you prepare at home for infants under twelve months.

After twelve months of age children still need much less salt than adults. It is not recommended that you add salt to food you prepare at home and you should check carefully the packaging of any foods your child is eating to see whether they contain high levels of salt.

Current Recommended Daily Maximum Intake (as recommended by the FSA)

- 1 to 3 years – 2g salt a day (0.8g sodium)
- 4 to 6 years – 3g salt a day (1.2g sodium)
- 7 to 10 years – 5g salt a day (2g sodium)
- 11 and over – 6g salt a day (2.4g sodium) – this is the same as the recommended levels for adults

Where Do I Find Salt on the Packaging?

There are three places to look for salt when shopping:

1. Ingredients list:
   Salt will be listed on the ingredients list. However, this does not really tell us exactly how much is in a product.

2. Nutritional Information:
   Salt and or sodium will be listed as follows:

	Typical amount per 100g
Sodium	g
of which sugars	g

3. Traffic Light labelling:
   Salt is one of the nutrients that is included in the Traffic Light labelling system. However, this and the guideline daily amounts are often just applicable to adults, and children's recommended amounts (if they are under eleven years old) are far less. Bear this mind, especially if a product has a high or red traffic light for salt for adults.

FIBRE

Fibre is one of the nutrients you may see listed in the nutritional information panel on packaging. It is also sometimes high-lighted as a nutrition claim on packaging if a product is high in fibre or is a source of fibre.

Fibre is basically another type of carbohydrate. It plays a vital role in helping the digestive system by keeping bowel movements regular.

There are two types of fibre:

1. **Soluble:**
   Found in fruits and vegetables, and oats. This type of fibre forms a gel when mixed with water. This can help lower the cholesterol in your blood as well as help you feel fuller.

2. **Insoluble:**
   Found in wholemeal bread, wholegrain breakfast cereals, brown rice and bran. We cannot digest this type of fibre so it passes through the digestive system and helps to bulk up our stools and reduce constipation.

Fibre and Children

Children aged five to fifteen years old should be getting about 15g of fibre per day.

Young children (under five years of age) in particular should not get too much insoluble fibre in their diet as this may fill their small tummies up and could mean they are unable to eat enough food each day to get the energy they need. Insoluble fibre can also prevent their bodies absorbing vital nutrients such as iron and calcium from the diet. Therefore, it is best not to give wholegrain varieties of all foods at every meal to very young children. For example, you could give them white pasta and rice or crumpets and muffins some of the time. Fruit and vegetables are fine.

By the time children are five years old they should be able to cope with greater amounts of fibre in their diet and eat in a similar way to the rest of the family.

Children need small amounts of each of the two types of fibre each day. Constipation can be a common problem in children of all ages. This can sometimes be helped by drinking more plain water and eating more fibre each day.

chapter 4

Adverse Reactions To Foods

INTRODUCTION
Adverse reactions cover many types of conditions, including acute food allergies and associated conditions such as anaphylactic shock, asthma, eczema and urticaria (skin reaction), diseases such as coeliac disease (allergy to gluten) as well as behavioural problems such as hyperactivity and Attention Deficit Hyperactivity Disorder (ADHD).

There has been some well-established scientific evidence produced that certain foods can trigger allergic reactions. This is why there are now regulations in place for the labelling of allergy information on packaging on twelve foods that have been cited as triggering allergic reactions (see Chapter 2, 'Allergy Information').

There has also been much research, some of which is inconclusive but some of which is more convincing, about the link between certain food additives and allergic reactions such as asthma, eczema and skin hives, and behavioural disorders from hyperactivity to the more severe ADHD.

If your child suffers from any of the above conditions, or if you think they may be at greater risk of developing them due to a strong family history, you may wish to take further precautions when planning their diet.

KEY ADDITIVES TO WATCH OUT FOR
I have based this list on up-to-date scientific evidence and current advice from the Food Standards Agency. In brackets I have listed how many of the 570 products I looked at contained that particular additive.

Food colours

E110   Sunset Yellow (5)
E104   Quinoline yellow (7)
E122   Carmoisine, Azorubine (6)
E129   Allura red (5)
E102   Tartrazine (0)

Reactions in a small number of people include asthma, hyper-activity and ADHD, urticaria (skin nettle rash), dermatitis (an allergic skin condition) and rhinitis (runny nose).

Sulphites

E220   Sulphur dioxide (10)
E221   Sodium sulphite (1)
E222   Sodium hydrogen sulphite (1)
E223   Sodium metabisulphite (17)
E224   Potassium metabisulphite (2)
E226   Calcium sulphite (1)
E227   Calcium hydrogen sulphite (1)
E228   Potassium hydrogen sulphite (1)

Reactions seen in a small number of people are asthma and hyperactivity.

Benzoates

E210   Benzoic acid (2)
E211   Sodium benzoate (6)
E212   Potassium benzoate (1)
E213   Calcium benzoate (1)
E214   Ethyl p-hydroxybenzoate (3)
E215   Sodium ethyl p-hydroxybenzoate (0)
E216   Propyl p-hydroxybenzoate (3)

E217   Sodium propyl p-hydroxybenzoate (0)
E218   Methyl p-hydroxybenzoate (3)
E219   Sodium methyl p-hydroxybenzoate (0)

Reactions seen in a small number of people are asthma, hyperactivity and eczema.

THE EUROPEAN FOOD SAFETY AUTHORITY (EFSA) REVIEW

The Food Standards Agency (FSA) has asked the EFSA to review the findings of research into some of the additives listed above. In addition, the EFSA are currently reviewing all food colourings permitted in foods. The results of this review are expected later this year (2008).

CHILDREN'S MEDICINES

When used in medicines, the following warnings have to be given on the labelling:

Colourings: E102 Tartrazine, E110 Sunset yellow, E122 Azorubine (Carmoisine), E123 Amaranth, E124 Ponceau 4R, E151 Brilliant black BN
Warning: May cause allergic reactions

Preservatives: E210 Benzoic acid, E211 Sodium benzoate, E212 Potassium benzoate
Warning: Mildly irritant to the skin, eyes and mucous membranes

Preservatives: E220 Sodium dioxide, E221 Sodium sulphite, E222 Sodium bisulphite, E223 Sodium metabisulphite, E224 Potassium metabisulphite and E228 Potassium bisulphite

Warning: May rarely cause severe hypersensitivity reactions and bronchospasm (difficulty in breathing).

USEFUL SOURCES OF FURTHER INFORMATION

- Allergy UK – www.allergyuk.org
- Asthma UK – www.asthma.org.uk
- National Eczema Society – www.eczema.org
- The Coeliac Society – www.coeliac.co.uk
- The Anaphylaxis Campaign – www.anaphylaxis.org.uk
- The Food Standards Agency advice – http://www.eatwell.gov.uk/foodlabels/understandingenumbers/ http://www.eatwell.gov.uk/healthissues/foodintolerance/foodintolerancetypes/foodadditiv/
- Action on Additives, for information on all foods containing the suspect additives – www.actiononadditives.com
- The Children's Hyperactivity Support Group – www.hacsg.org.uk

CHILDREN'S HYPERACTIVITY SUPPORT GROUP: RECOMMENDED ADDITIVES TO AVOID

This organisation provides support to parents and professionals working with children who display signs of hyperactivity, with particular focus on the nutritional factors. They recommend that affected children should avoid the following additives:

COLOURS

E102 Tartrazine
E104 Quinoline yellow
E110 Sunset yellow
E122 Carmoisine; Azorubine
E123 Amaranth
E124 Ponceau 4R or Cochineal Red A
E127 Erythrosine B5
E128 Red 2G
E129 Allura red AC
E131 Patent blue V
E132 Indigo carmine; Indigotine
E133 Brilliant blue FCF
E142 Green S
E150 Caramel (a) (b) (c) (d)

E151 Black PN; Brilliant black BN
E154 Brown FK
E155 Brown HT
E161 (g) Canthaxanthin
E173 Aluminium
E180 Litholrubine BK; Pigment
    rubine

FLAVOURINGS

All except where stated as
natural should be avoided. They
do not have E numbers.

FLAVOUR ENHANCERS

E621 Monosodium glutamate
    (MSG)
E622 Monopotassium glutamate
    (MPG)

ANTIOXIDANTS

E320 Butylated hydroxy anisole
    (BHA)
E321 Butylated hydroxy toluene
    (BHT)

PRESERVATIVES

E210 Benzoic acid
E211 Sodium benzoate
E220 Sulphur dioxide
E282 Calcium propionate
Sulphites:
E221 Sodium sulphite
E222 Sodium hydrogen sulphite
E223 Sodium metabisulphite
E224 Potassium metabisulphite
E226 Calcium sulphite
E227 Calcium bisulphite
E228 Potassium hydrogen
    sulphite

Other preservatives:
E212 Potassium benzoate
E213 Calcium benzoate
E214 Ethyl p-hydroxybenzoate
E215 Sodium ethyl p-hydroxyben-
    zoate
E216 Propyl p-hydroxybenzoate
E217 Sodium propyl p-hydroxy-
    benzoate
E218 Methyl p-hydroxybenzoate
E219 Sodium methyl p-hydroxy-
    benzoate
E230 Diphenyl
E231 Ortho phenylphenol
E232 Sodium orthophylphenate
E233 Thiabendazode
E234 Nisin
E235 Natamycin

ADDITIVES NOT PERMITTED IN INFANT FOODS AND WEANING FOODS:
ANTIOXIDANTS
E310 Propyl gallate
E311 Octyl gallate
E312 Dodecyl gallate

SWEETENERS

E950 Acesulfame
E951 Aspartame
E953 Isomalt
E954 Saccharin
E965 (i) (ii) Maltol
E966 Lactitol
E967 Xylitol

chapter 5

Manufacturers' Claims: What Do They Really Mean?

This chapter looks at some of the nutritional and health claims, as well as other statements used on packaging aimed at children and their parents, that I found on the products I looked at in my survey.

Since July 2007 any nutrition (e.g. 'source of fibre', 'low in salt') and health (e.g. 'helps maintain a healthy heart', 'helps aid digestion') claims are now regulated by European legislation. Any other statements on packaging that do not fall into these categories should not be false or misleading but are not regulated specifically by legislation.

SOME OF THE NUTRITION CLAIMS I FOUND

When a manufacturer makes a nutrition-based claim they are then under legal obligation to provide a nutrition information breakdown on the packaging to substantiate this. The Food Standards Agency provides guidelines for manufacturers for when making such claims.

Source of Calcium

To be able to make a declaration about a vitamin or mineral it must be present in a 'significant' amount. Significant amount means 15 per cent or more of the Recommended Daily Allowance per 100g, per 100ml or per portion if the package contains only one portion. The calcium can be present naturally in that product or may have been added specifically to enrich it with calcium. Claims like this do not mean the product is anything other than a source of calcium. They do not mean that it is a 'healthy' product or that it is low in sugar, fat or salt.

High in Vitamin C
To use the word 'high' the product should supply 30 per cent of the Recommended Daily Allowance per 100g, per 100ml or per portion if the package contains only one portion. The vitamin C can be present naturally in the product or may have been added specifically to enrich it in vitamin C. As with the calcium, claims like this do not make the product anything other than a rich source of vitamin C. They do not mean that it is a 'healthy' product or that it is low in sugar, fat or salt.

One of Your '5 a Day'
This is referring to the advice that we all should have five portions of different fruit and vegetables a day. Some labels highlight that consuming their product will count towards this. Common products making such claims include fruit juices and smoothies, ready-meals and dried-fruit snack bars.

However, keep in mind that drinking two fruit-juice drinks a day does not mean you have consumed two of your five portions. Fruit juice, no matter how much is drunk, or how many different types are consumed, can only count as one portion a day. The same rule applies to pulses, for example beans, lentils and chickpeas, which cannot count as more than one portion a day.

It is always wise to check labels to see if the product is suitable in other ways – a ready-meal may have vegetables counting as one portion but may also be a high source of salt. Dried-fruit bars may offer your child one way of getting some fruit but this comes in the form of quite concentrated fruit sugars and can often contain added sugars too. Nothing beats eating fresh or frozen fruit and vegetables.

Fortified with Vitamins and Iron

This means that certain vitamins and iron have been added to the product, which might not otherwise be a source of these nutrients. The body will see no difference between these added nutrients and those present naturally in a product. This can be a good way of increasing your child's intake of vitamins and minerals each day. However, do check the full nutritional information and ingredients lists, as these products may not necessarily be totally healthy (e.g. many breakfast cereals have added vitamins but are also high in sugar).

Low Fat

To make this claim the product should contain less than 3g of fat per 100g or per 100ml of a product. Many products are naturally this low in fat. Others have been reformulated by the manufacturer to create a low-fat version. In this case check for things like sugar and salt, which may be present in higher amounts to replace the taste of the fat. Sometimes a low-fat product may not be thought of as 'healthy' (many sweets are naturally low in fat).

SOME OF THE OTHER STATEMENTS I FOUND

No Artificial Colours or Flavourings

More and more products now have this claim and it is commendable that so many manufacturers are voluntarily choosing to remove the artificial colourings and flavourings from so many foods. However, as I have pointed out earlier, these claims do not mean a product is automatically suitable for children or 'healthy'. A food may still be high in fat, saturated fat or sugar. Also ask yourself what is left off the statement, especially if your child is sensitive to certain additives – for example, 'no colourings or flavourings' makes no mention of preservatives, so it may still contain a number of these – always read the ingredients list.

Wholegrain

This is a term that is also becoming more widely used, especially with products containing cereals (wheat, oats, rice, etc.) such as breakfast cereals and breads. Wholegrain means that only the inedible part of the grain (the husk or shell) has been removed by processing, leaving the entire germ and bran parts.

By keeping most of the grain intact, wholegrain is a source of both fibre and a number of essential nutrients, vitamins and minerals. When the cereal grain has been processed further and other parts of the grain removed, for example the bran parts, then the product ceases to be classed as wholegrain. This applies for products such as white breads, white-flour products and non-wholegrain breakfast cereals. These are typically lower in fibre and nutrients than the wholegrain varieties.

Wholegrains are harder for our bodies to digest than more processed versions of the same grains so this means they digest more slowly and provide a more lasting energy than the more processed versions.

Note: Wholegrain foods are not automatically high in fibre as some grains contain more fibre than others.

Products that use grain from which parts like bran have been removed, but which have subsequently had bran added to them, are not able to be classed as using wholegrain. This is the case of brown bread that is made using wheat flour rather than wholemeal flour and then usually has some bran added to the bread too – this gives it a browner colour but does not make it wholegrain.

Currently there are no legal definitions specifying how much of a product has to be a wholegrain cereal for it to be classed as 'wholegrain'. In the meantime, it is always best to check the ingredients list and look for the words 'wholemeal', 'whole' or 'wholegrain' preceding the cereal name. If these ingredients are the first listed or near the beginning it is likely that the product is a good source of wholegrains and should provide the associated nutritional benefits.

Great for Lunchboxes

This has no legal meaning and parents should not be mistaken that the product is suitable or healthy for children. In many of the instances in which I found this claim had been made, it seemed to refer to the fact that items were individually wrapped and no more.

Endorsed by Nutritionists

This does not really have any legal definition as such or mean that a product follows regulations set by the FSA. It merely means that a particular manufacturer or retailer has a nutritionist working on board (as they all do) who has declared the product as meeting internally set guidelines. This is obviously a great marketing tool aimed at parents.

This is not to imply that these types of claims are meaningless or dubious. However, the precise nutritional information of an individual product should always be looked at before making assumptions about a product's nutritional value.

Strict Limits on Sugar, Fat, Saturated Fat and Salt

Some children's ranges make these types of statement about how they have limited the sugar, saturated fat or salt content of a product. This does not mean these products meet any legally set regulations by the FSA for children's foods, as none exist. It just means the manufacturer or retailer has looked at the product range and decided on its own guidelines. This is probably as much a marketing tool as a move to help the health of our children. However, on the whole, these ranges scored well in my analysis.

No Added Sugar

This usually means that the food or drink has not had any sugar added to it as an ingredient. It does not necessarily mean that a product does not contain any naturally occurring sugars or that it does not still taste sweet due to the addition of sweeteners. As a parent it is still important to read the ingredients list and check for any nutritional information, particularly if you would like to be careful about giving your child high-sugar products or those containing sweeteners.

Sugar is a natural preservative and in my analysis I saw greater use of preservatives such as sodium metabisulphite and sodium benzoate in drinks that had no added sugar or were specifically described as sugar free.

Unsweetened

This usually means that no sugar or sweeteners have been added to the product to make it taste sweet. It may still taste sweet or have some sugars from naturally occurring sources such as fruit sugars.

Nutritious

Though it sounds great, this term does not have any legal definition and, because it is making no real nutritional claim as such, it does not fall under any guidelines. Such terms are a great marketing tool but may not actually mean a product offers anything of nutritional benefit to the body.

Nutritionally Balanced

I couldn't find any reference to what this term means legally in the food regulations and guidelines that are available. In law, any claim that in some way refers to the nutritional benefit of a product cannot be misleading or false, but whether it means anything specific is doubtful. It is a term used by many manufacturers and retailers on the products I looked at and can be taken to mean that the products in some way fit the broad healthy-eating guidelines set by the Department of Health (that state our diets should contain a certain proportion of carbohydrates, proteins, fats, etc., whilst restricting the quantities of salt, sugar and fat). The claim also does not necessarily mean that a product is nutritionally balanced for *children*. However, as always, my advice is that if you are in any doubt, check individual packets for the nutrition information and ingredients lists.

Contains Real Fruit Juice

This basically means that the product contains some fruit juice. This is also true of any product that contains fruit-juice concentrates. Unfortunately, it does not seem to guarantee how much fruit juice a product contains, and in my analysis the average amount of fruit juice in a product making such a claim was only 6 per cent.

Contains Real Fruit Purée

As above, this means that the product contains some real fruit that has been puréed, but does not offer any guarantee of exact amounts and, again, the average content in products making this claim was 6 per cent.

Packed with Goodness

Sounds great, but does not have a legal definition.

Honest, Tasty, Real
Again, sounds great, but these do not have a legal or nutritional definition.

Contains 50 per cent Fruit
This and other such percentages is a popular one on fruit drinks and dried fruit and cereal bars. It does not, however, mean that the other 50 per cent of the product is as virtuous and does not mean that the product is not also high in concentrated fruit sugars.

Healthy Snack for Kids
This does not have a legal definition and is likely to be on a packet as a marketing tool, so judge the product on its ingredients list and nutritional information first and foremost.

Multigrain
This is often listed on breakfast cereals or bread products. It simply means that more than one cereal grain can be found in the product e.g. wheat, rice, corn, oats. This does not indicate that a product is wholegrain or wholemeal, or healthier than a product that just has one cereal grain

chapter 6

A–Z Reference Guide

HOW TO USE THE REFERENCE GUIDE

- This is an alphabetical list of all the ingredients and additives that I found in 570 children's foods, beverages and children's medicines. It is not a comprehensive guide of all ingredients and additives that are used in the food industry.
- **What is it?** This is a simple non-technical explanation of the ingredient or additive.
- **Further Information:** where relevant, further information including the nutritional composition of an ingredient and possible adverse reactions to an additive. This also includes how many products I found specific additives in and what types of products these were.
- **E Number:** I have also listed, where relevant, the E number.
- Words in italics means that they are also to be found in the guide.
- Where the term 'source of' has been used, this means a food provides 10–20 per cent of the RDA; where the term 'good source' is used, this means 20–30 per cent of the RDA is provided; where the term 'rich source' is used, this means the food provides at least 30 per cent of the RDA.

INGREDIENT	WHAT IS IT?	FURTHER INFORMATION
Acacia gum **E414**	This is a type of gum extracted from the African acacia tree. It can also be known as gum arabic. It has many uses including a *thickener, stabiliser, emulsifier* and *glazing agent*. Acacia gum can also help stop sugar from crystallising.	Research studies in humans looking at acacia gum and asthma and skin irritability have been few and inconclusive. This additive is permitted in organic foods. For more information about organic foods see Chapter 2 and Appendix 2.
Acesulfame K **E950**	This is an artificial sweetener. It is 200 times sweeter than table sugar but is calorie free as it passes through the body undigested. It is one of a group of intense sweeteners used in food and drinks. For more information about sweeteners see Chapter 2. It is very bitter and is therefore usually used in combination with other low-calorie sweeteners. It is used in low-sugar or diet products such as drinks and sweets. It is also known as acesulfame potassium.	I found this sweetener in 7 out of 570 products that I looked at. These were all sugar-free drinks. Though a link between this sweetener and hyperactivity has not been scientifically proven, this is one of the artificial sweeteners that the Children's Hyperactivity Support Group recommend is avoided in sensitive children's diets. For more information see Chapter 4.
Acetic acid **E260**	This is an acid that occurs naturally in a variety of fruits and plants. It is also the main constitute of vinegar. It is used for preserving foods	

INGREDIENT	WHAT IS IT?	FURTHER INFORMATION
	and flavouring foods. It has antibacterial functions and is also used by manufacturers as an *acidity regulator*.	
Acetic acid esters of mono- and diglycerides of fatty acids E472a	Made from *acetic acid* and used as an *emulsifier*. It is also used to stabilise and modify the texture of foods.	
Acidity regulator	These are substances that help control the level of acidity in a food or drink. For example, they help maintain the sharp acidic flavour of lemonade. As a group they include acids, alkalis and neutralising agents. There are approximately 35 different ones used by food manufacturers. Usually the specific name is listed in brackets.	
Adipic acid E355	Adipic acid is found naturally in some plants but is made synthetically for food production use. It is used to increase the acidic flavour of a food or as a *raising agent*.	
Adzuki beans	This is a dark red bean that comes from an Asian plant. It is sweet-tasting and the basis for Cantonese red-bean paste used in Chinese cooking.	These beans are a source of *vegetarian protein* as well as sources of *iron, zinc, vitamin B1* and *niacin* and *dietary fibre*.
Agave nectar/syrup	This is a sugar syrup which comes from the South American	It has a lower *glycaemic index (GI)* than table sugar or golden

INGREDIENT	WHAT IS IT?	FURTHER INFORMATION
	agave plant (the same plant tequila is made from). It can be used to sweeten foods or in place of golden syrup to help hold flapjack or fruit and cereal bars together. It is sweeter than sugar to taste.	syrup and so it digests more slowly and does not cause such a rise in blood-sugar levels and the associated energy highs and lows.
Alaskan pollock	This is a white fish now used more commonly to replace cod in foods such as fish fingers.	This is a source of protein.
Allura red E129	This is a water-soluble artificial food colourant. It is used to give foods a reddish-yellow colour. It is one of the group of *azo dyes* permitted in food use.	This is one of five food colourants which the Food Standards Agency in the UK is currently recommending should be avoided if your child shows symptoms of hyperactivity. For more information see Chapter 2 (Colourings).
		This is one of the food additives currently under review by the European Food Safety Authority. This may lead to a change in regulation sometime in 2008. For updated information about this food dye see the website www.whatsinthis.co.uk.
		I found it in 5 out of the 570 products I looked at and these were all cake mixes and sweets.
Almonds	These are one of the most widely grown nuts and are used in a variety of sweet and savoury dishes, e.g. curries and marzipan. Ground almond is also sometimes used in cake baking.	Almonds are a source of protein as well as *niacin*, vitamin B2, *vitamin E, iron, zinc* and *dietary fibre*. They are about 35% *fat* of which 10% is saturated and 70% monounsaturated.

INGREDIENT	WHAT IS IT?	FURTHER INFORMATION
Alpha tocopherol E307	This is a synthetically made version of *vitamin E*. It is added to foods as an *antioxidant*.	*Vitamin E* is an important vitamin for the body.
Ammonia caramel E150c	This is a natural food colouring and one of four caramel colourants produced by heating carbohydrates (e.g. sugars or malt syrups) in the presence of small amounts of food-grade acids, alkalis or salts. These colours are the most commonly used colourants in food and drinks. Caramel is also used in flavourings.	Research into this food colourant and a link to asthma and skin irritation has not been scientifically conclusive. However, this is one of the food colours the Children's Hyperactivity Support Group recommends is avoided by sensitive children. I found this food colour in just over 60% of the products I looked at which contained food colours.
Ammonium bicarbonate/ Ammonium hydrogen carbonate E503	This is made synthetically and is used as a *raising agent* in breads and many baked products.	This additive is permitted in organic foods. For more information about organic foods see Chapter 2 and Appendix 2.
Ammonium phosphatides E442	This is used as an *emulsifier*. Used commonly in chocolate products. It is a mixture of *glycerin* and *rapeseed oil*.	I found this in many of the chocolate products I looked at.
Anhydrous milk fat	This is *milk fat* with a very high *fat* content and negligible water content. (Anhydrous means free of water.)	
Annatto E160b	This is a natural food colouring that comes from the seeds of the tropical tree *Bixa orellana*. It produces a yellowish-red colour. It is used in products such as	I found annatto was used in about 60% of the products containing natural food colours. It was listed on one own-brand ice-cream product that

83

INGREDIENT	WHAT IS IT?	FURTHER INFORMATION
	cheese, margarines and fish. It is often used as a natural alternative food colouring to the artificial azo food colour Tartrazine (E102).	it has been associated with food intolerance. It is also one of the food colours that the Children's Hyperactivity Support Group recommends is avoided by sensitive children. However there seems to be no real scientific evidence for its association with hyperactivity. This is an additive permitted in organic foods for use in specific cheeses e.g. Double Gloucester and Red Leicester. For more information about organic foods see Chapter 2 and Appendix 2.
Anthocyanins E163	This is a food colouring derived from natural plant pigments. Usually used to give foods a red and blue or reddish/blue colour. It is found naturally in red grapes, red cabbage and elderberries.	I found this used commonly when a product specified natural colours. Used in a wide range of products from yogurts to drinks, sweets and biscuits.
Anti-caking agent	These additives are added to fine powders or crystalline foods to prevent them clumping, e.g. icing sugar, custard powders. The specific name should be listed in brackets.	
Antioxidant	These are a group of substances added to foods to stop them oxidising, i.e. being affected by exposure to air and going rancid or discolouring. The most commonly used food antioxidants are BHA butylated hydroxyanisole and BHT (butylated hydroxytoluene).	Foods possessing high antioxidative activity are associated with a number of health benefits.

INGREDIENT	WHAT IS IT?	FURTHER INFORMATION
	Naturally occurring antioxidant compounds include *ascorbic acid* (*vitamin C*) and *tocopherols* (*vitamin E*).	
Apple	When apple is listed on the ingredients list it means that whole apple has gone into the product.	Apples contain *dietary fibre* and *vitamin C*.
Apple extracts	See *Fruit extracts*.	
Apple juice from concentrate	See *Fruit juice from concentrate*.	
Apple vinegar	Also known as cider vinegar. This is when vinegar is produced from fermented apples.	
Apricot	This is a type of fruit.	Apricots are a source of *vitamin A*, *vitamin C* and some *dietary fibre*. Dried apricots are a source of *niacin*, *iron* and *dietary fibre*.
Arborio rice	This is a type of rice used commonly in risotto dishes and paella. It has a higher starch content than standard rice and so it thickens more when cooked and sticks together better.	
Aronia	This is a berry fruit with is a violet-black colour. It is used as a source of juice in foods and also may be used to impart colour or flavour to foods or beverages.	Aronia berries are high in *antioxidants* and *vitamin C*.

INGREDIENT	WHAT IS IT?	FURTHER INFORMATION
Aronia juice from concentrate	See *Fruit juice from concentrate* and *aronia*.	
Ascorbic acid E300	Ascorbic acid is another name for *vitamin C*. It is a natural preservative and is used to help prolong shelf life and freshness of foods. It is used to stop foods discolouring and going rancid when they are exposed to air. It is found naturally occurring in many foods.	When used in the food industry it is often synthetically produced but still imparts the health benefits of the natural substance. This additive is permitted in organic foods. For more information about organic foods see Chapter 2 and Appendix 2.
Ascorbyl palmitate E304	This is a mix of *ascorbic acid (vitamin C)* and palmitic acid (a natural fat) and is used as a preservative. Mixing ascorbic acid with palmitic acid creates a form of vitamin C that is fat-soluble, i.e. it can be transported into the body in fat so can be used to preserve foods which have a high fat content.	
Aspartame E951	Aspartame is an artificial sweetener used in low-sugar or diet products. It is 160–200 times sweeter than sugar and is used in very tiny amounts, therefore providing fewer calories than sugar-containing equivalents. It is non-cariogenic, i.e. it is not harmful for teeth.	There has been some research linking aspartame to headaches, depression, anxiety and hyperactivity, as well as carcinogenic concerns. However, the published research does not seem to substantiate any of these. I found aspartame in 8 out of 570 products. These were all sugar-free drinks and cordials. See also *phenylalanine*.

INGREDIENT	WHAT IS IT?	FURTHER INFORMATION
Aspartame-acesulfame/ acesulphame E950/E951	This is a mix of the two chemical sweeteners *aspartame* and *acesulfame K*. It is 350 times sweeter than table sugar.	
Avocado	This is a fruit of a tree also known as an avocado pear. It is used in salads or to make guacamole (a puréed dip). It is rich in *vitamin E* and *polyunsaturated* oils.	It has a high fat content (approximately 26%). It is a source of polyunsaturated fat and is a rich source of *vitamin C* and a good source of *vitamin B6* and a source of protein and *iron*.
Azo dyes	These are a group of artificial food colourants. They are called 'azo' because chemically they contain something called an 'azo' group.	
Azorubine E122	This is an artificial food colouring permitted in food use, which gives foods a blueish-red colour. It is also known as *carmoisine*.	This is one of five food colourants that the Food Standards Agency in the UK is currently recommending should be avoided if your child shows symptoms of hyperactivity. For more information see Chapter 2 (Colourings). This is one of the food additives currently under review by the European Food Safety Authority. This may lead to a change in regulation sometime in 2008. For updated information about this food dye see the website www.whatsinthis.co.uk. I found it in 7 out of the 570 products I looked at and these were yogurts and yogurt drinks, brightly coloured confectionery, cake decorations, cake mixes and jelly.

INGREDIENT	WHAT IS IT?	FURTHER INFORMATION
Baby-grade vegetables	This is a term used to describe when vegetables have been grown specially by a food manufacturer for use in baby purées and weaning foods. This specific term does not have a legal meaning. However, current legislation limits pesticide types and amounts of residue in these products and products aimed at infants under 12 months.	
Balsamic vinegar	This is a vinegar made from grape juice.	
Banana	This is a type of fruit.	Bananas are a good source of *vitamin A* and are a source of *vitamin B6* and *vitamin C*. They also contain *dietary fibre*.
Barley	This is a cereal. It contains gluten so should be avoided by anyone with coeliac disease. The whole barley grains are known as pearl barley and are sometimes used as an ingredient in soups and casseroles. *Malt* is an ingredient used in food and beverages and can come from barley.	Barley is a source of *niacin*, *vitamin B6*, *folate*, *zinc* and *iron* and provides some *dietary fibre*. I found it used in multigrain products and some breakfast cereals. It is used commonly in livestock feeds and beer production.

INGREDIENT	WHAT IS IT?	FURTHER INFORMATION
Barley flour	This is the ground-down version of *barley* grains. It is sometimes used as a *bulking agent* in foods.	
Barley malt flavouring	*Malt* can be produced from the *barley* grain and is commonly used in foods to naturally enhance flavour and colour.	I found this in breakfast cereals.
Barley malt vinegar flavouring	*Malt* can be derived from the *barley* grain and is used as a flavour and also fermented to make vinegar. This is also used as a natural flavouring added to foods.	
Basil extract	Basil is a herb used to flavour foods. Basil extract is produced by grinding dried basil and then extracting the oil, which is very concentrated in flavour. This is added to foods for flavour.	
Basil oil	Basil is a herb used to flavour foods. Basil oil is produced when fresh basil leaves are ground to a paste and the oil is extracted.	
Basmati rice	This is a long-grain Indian variety of rice.	It has a lower *glycaemic index (GI)* than normal rice so it digests more slowly and can help balance blood-sugar and energy levels. For more information about the Glycaemic Index see Chapter 2.

INGREDIENT	WHAT IS IT?	FURTHER INFORMATION
Bay leaf (extract)	These are leaves from the bay tree, used in cooking to add flavour to a dish. Manufacturers use the extract of them, i.e. the oil, to add flavour.	
Béchamel sauce	Also known as white sauce. It is made with butter, wheat flour and milk. Sometimes also made with cheese.	
Beef	Where this appears in the ingredients list it means that real beef meat has been used.	Beef meat is a rich source of protein, *niacin*, *iron* and *vitamin B12*. It is 20–30% *fat* of which about half is saturated *fat*.
Beef collagen casings	Collagen casings are commonly used to wrap around sausages. Beef collagen is found in the skin of cows.	
Beef extract	This is dried beef meat that has been ground to a powder form.	
Beef fat	This is when just the fat from beef meat is used.	
Beef gelatine	This is used as a *thickener* or *emulsifier* and is a substance found in cows' bones and skin.	
Beeswax E901	This is used as a *glazing agent* and is obtained from bees or synthetically made.	
Beetroot juice	Juice from beetroots, which can be used as a sweetener or to add colour to foods and drinks.	
Beetroot red E162	This is a natural food colouring derived from the beetroot	I found it in yogurts, sweets and drinks.

INGREDIENT	WHAT IS IT?	FURTHER INFORMATION
	vegetable. Also known as *betanin*.	
Bell peppers	These are a large bell-shaped sweet-tasting fruit found in the vegetable sections of supermarkets. They come in a variety of colours from green to yellow and red depending on the stage of ripeness. *Capsicum* is also another name for them.	Bell peppers are a rich source of *vitamin C* and also contain some *dietary fibre*.
Beta-apo-8′-carotenal E160e	This is a natural food colour extracted from plants – it gives an orange to yellow colour.	
Beta-carotene E160a	This is a natural food colouring. It is extracted from plants such as carrots, tomatoes, oranges and spinach. It is also the vegetable source of *vitamin A* and is a natural *antioxidant*.	This is one I found used in many products from drinks, sweets, yogurts, cheese, ready-meals, ice cream and lollies.
Betanin E162	This is a colour pigment found in beetroots. It is used as a natural food colouring. It is also known as *beetroot red*.	
Bifido probiotic cultures	Commonly added to yogurt products, these are naturally occurring bacteria found in a number of foods and in everyone's bodies.	Adding them to foods is done as this may help maintain a healthy digestive system. Products containing these bacteria cultures are regarded as Functional Foods. For more information about Functional Foods see Chapter 2.
Blackcurrant extracts	See *fruit extracts*.	

INGREDIENT	WHAT IS IT?	FURTHER INFORMATION
Blackcurrant juice from concentrate	See *fruit juice from concentrate*.	
Black pepper	These are small berries which are dried and ground to produce black pepper. Used to add flavour to food.	
Bleached flour	This is when ground wheat is chemically bleached to make it whiter in appearance or improve its baking quality.	
Bovine collagen casing	This is when collagen (a substance found in cows' skins) is used to wrap sausages.	
Bran	This is the outer layer of cereal grains such as wheat. In *wholegrain* products such as pasta and bread the bran part is left intact on the grain. When preparing white flour and white rice, etc., this layer is removed. This outer layer known as bran can also be added to foods as an ingredient.	Bran is a source of nutrients including *niacin, zinc, iron, vitamin B1* and vitamin B2 and *dietary fibre*.
Brazil nuts	These nuts grow on trees. They are sometimes found in breakfast cereals, muesli and cereal bars.	Brazil nuts are a very rich source of selenium, a rich source of *vitamin B1* and *vitamin E*, and a good source of protein, *niacin* and calcium. They are about 40% *fat* of which 25% is saturated and 40% is monounsaturated.
Brilliant black BN; Black PN E151	This is an artificial food colouring that imparts a black colour to foods.	No supposed links to asthma, hyperactivity, allergic reactions and skin reactions have been

INGREDIENT	WHAT IS IT ?	FURTHER INFORMATION
		scientifically proven. However, it is one of the food colours recommended by the Children's Hyperactivity Support Group be avoided in diets of sensitive children. I found it in 1 product out of 570, which was a yogurt drink.
Brilliant blue FCF E133	This is an artificial food colouring that imparts a greenish-blue tint to foods.	No supposed links to asthma, hyperactivity, allergic reactions and skin reactions have been scientifically proven. However, it is one of the food colours recommended by the Children's Hyperactivity Support Group be avoided in diets of sensitive children. I found it in 3 products, which were cake mixes and sweets and chocolate confectionery.
Brown rice	When the outer husk (protective coat) of the rice grain has been removed you are left with brown rice. This has the outer bran layers still intact. Standard white rice is when the outer skin has been removed.	Brown rice is a good source of *niacin* and a source of protein, *vitamin B1* and selenium as well as *dietary fibre*.
Brown rice syrup	This is used as a sweetener in foods and also as an alternative to golden syrup. It is made from fermenting brown rice and has the consistency of honey.	It is about 20% as sweet as table sugar and is a lower-sugar option for sweetening children's foods. I found it in a number of cereal bars.
Brown sugar	This is granulated white sugar which has had some *molasses* added to it to give it the brown	

INGREDIENT	WHAT IS IT?	FURTHER INFORMATION
	colour. Brown sugar should not be confused with *raw sugar* and *unrefined sugar*. It may be classed as light or dark depending on how much molasses has been added to it.	
Buckwheat/ buckwheat flakes	Buckwheat is a cereal grain. It is gluten free and so most commonly used in wheat-free and gluten-free products in its flour or flake forms. It can be used in breakfast cereals, breads and cakes. It is also used to make the little Russian pancakes called blinis and Japanese soba noodles.	Buckwheat is a source of *protein*, *niacin*, *vitamin B1* and vitamin B2. I found it in gluten-free products.
Buffered lactic acid E270	Lactic acid is produced by the fermentation of carbohydrates and was originally discovered in soured milk. It is what gives the flavour to fermented milk. Buffered lactic acid is used in confectionery to help produce a really clear sweet and is used to improve the taste in many soft drinks.	I found this in some sweets.
Bulking agent	These help add bulk to a product without adding lots of calories. They are often used to simulate more expensive ingredients. They are commonly used in meat products such as sausages. These will be listed by their specific names.	
Butter	This is made by churning the fat separated from milk until it hardens to form butter. Legally it	Due to its high saturated *fat* content (60% of the fat is saturated) it is recommended

INGREDIENT	WHAT IS IT?	FURTHER INFORMATION
	has to be no less than 80% fat to be called butter.	that children consume butter in moderation.
Butter fat	This appears on the ingredients list when just the fat from butter has been used in the product.	
Buttermilk	Traditionally this is the liquid left after churning butter. Nowadays buttermilk is more likely to be made by adding *lactic acid* to milk to simulate buttermilk.	
Buttermilk powder	When *buttermilk* has the water content removed to turn it into powder form.	
Butter oil	A milk-fat product which is no less than 90% fat.	
Butylated hydroxyanisole (BHA) E320	This is a synthetic fat-soluble *antioxidant*. It is used in high-fat foods as a preservative and remains stable when heated.	

INGREDIENT	WHAT IS IT?	FURTHER INFORMATION
Caffeine	Caffeine is a naturally occurring stimulant found in coffee beans, tea leaves and chocolate (cocoa beans). It is therefore found in all products derived from these, e.g. chocolate-containing products.	It is best to keep caffeine consumption to a minimum in children. Too much may cause headaches, stomach upset, diarrhoea and difficulty sleeping.
	It is also added to certain foods, e.g. cola drinks, including low-sugar varieties, energy drinks and some medicines.	
	It raises blood pressure, stimulates the kidneys and temporarily averts fatigue and tiredness.	
Calcium carbonate E170	This is a chemical compound found naturally in some rocks like chalk, marble and limestone.	Calcium is an important nutrient for the body. See page 45.
	It is used as a *firming agent* and a source of dietary *calcium*.	This is an additive permitted in organic foods. For more information about organic foods see Chapter 2 and Appendix 2.
Calcium chloride E509	This is a salt used as a firming agent and to preserve flavour in foods.	This is an additive permitted in organic foods. For more information about organic foods see Chapter 2 and Appendix 2.
Calcium citrate E333	This is a natural source of calcium. Used as an *acidity regulator*.	This additive is permitted in organic foods. For more information about organic foods see Chapter 2 and Appendix 2.

INGREDIENT	WHAT IS IT?	FURTHER INFORMATION
Calcium hydrogen sulphite E227	This is one of a group of *sulphites* that are used as food *preservatives*. If a product contains sulphites at levels above 10mg per kg this legally has to be labelled on the product.	Sulphites have been scientifically proven to be able to trigger asthma so they are best avoided if your child suffers from asthma. This additive is also one recommended by the Children's Hyperactivity Support Group to be avoided by sensitive children.
Calcium lactate E327	This is the calcium salt of *lactic acid*. This is used to affect the acidity of a food or drink or act as a *preservative*.	
Calcium phosphate E341	This is used as a *firming agent* or *raising agent* in foods. Also known as *monocalcium phosphate*.	Used as an ingredient in baking powder and self-raising flour.
Calcium propionate E282	While this is found naturally in some cheeses, it is manufactured commercially for use by the food industry. It is used as a *preservative* as it inhibits mould growth. Common in breads and baked goods such as crumpets, rolls and buns.	Though some links have been proposed between calcium propionate and migraines, headaches, skin rashes, irritability, aggression or hyperactivity in some sensitive children, this has not been scientifically proven. I found this to be used only in baked products such as breads and it was found in 6 out of 15 products looked at.
Calcium stearoyl-2-lactate E482	This is used as an *emulsifier* and is derived from *lactic acid*.	

INGREDIENT	WHAT IS IT?	FURTHER INFORMATION
Calcium sulphate/ sulphite E226	This is one of a group of *sulphites* that are used as food *preservatives*. If a product contains sulphites at levels above 10mg per kg this legally has to be labelled on the product.	Sulphites have been scientifically proven to be able to trigger asthma so they are best avoided if your child suffers from asthma. This additive is also one recommended by the Children's Hyperactivity Support Group to be avoided by sensitive children.
Camelina seed oil	This is a natural oil derived from the seeds of the camelina plant. It is used by manufacturers as it is a stable oil and does not deteriorate with storage.	It is a source of polyunsaturated *fats* and is low in saturated fat.
Cane sugar	This is a *sugar* that comes from processing the stalks of the sugar cane plant.	Cane sugar has no nutrients for the body other than calories. It is cariogenic, i.e. encourages dental caries/ fillings.
Capsicum (extract)	Capsicum is another name for peppers, which includes *bell peppers*, *paprika* and *chillies*. Sometimes used as a natural food colouring or flavouring.	
Caramel E150a E150b E150c E150d	There are 4 different caramel colourants used by food manufacturers ranging from light brown to very dark brown in colour. They are produced by heating carbohydrates (e.g. sugars or malt syrups) in the presence of small amounts of food-grade acids, alkalis or salts.	See also *plain* caramel E150a, *caustic sulphite caramel* E150b, *ammonia caramel* E150c and sulphite ammonia caramel E150d.

INGREDIENT	WHAT IS IT?	FURTHER INFORMATION
	These colours are the most commonly used colourants in food. Caramel is also used in *flavourings*.	
Caramelised sugar	This is when *sugar* is carefully heated until it thickens and takes on a caramel flavour and colour. It may also be used as a *thickener* in foods and drinks.	
Caramelised syrup	This is made by carefully heating *sugar* until it caramelises and produces a caramel flavour and colour.	
Carbohydrate	Carbohydrates are a type of food that supplies us with energy. All carbohydrate foods are broken down (digested) in our bodies into glucose, which provides us with blood sugar and is used by every cell in our bodies for energy. Carbohydrates provide the body with 4 calories per gram.	For more information see Chapter 3: What Every Parent Should Know About Children's Nutrition.
Carbonated water	This is when water has had carbon dioxide gas dissolved into it to make it fizzy. The process is called carbonation. Carbon dioxide is the gas our bodies produce naturally when we breathe in oxygen and then breathe out carbon dioxide.	There have been some concerns over the consuming of large quantities of fizzy water and weakening bones or stomach problems but these claims have not really been founded in good research studies. Drinking lots of fizzy drinks may cause a child to have a bit of extra gas/flatulence in their stomach, which can sometimes cause a stomach ache.

INGREDIENT	WHAT IS IT?	FURTHER INFORMATION
Carbon black; vegetable carbon E153	This is a black food colouring that comes from burning plant material.	I found this food colouring in 2 products out of 570; a cake mix and a variety of confectionery.
		This is one additive permitted in organic foods. (For more information about organic foods see Chapter 2 and Appendix 2.)
Carboxy methyl cellulose E466	Created chemically, this additive has many uses including as a *stabiliser*, a *thickener* and *bulking agent*.	
Carmines E120	This is a natural food colour derived from *cochineal* (an insect). It is a deep red colour. Also called *carminic acid*.	10 products out of 570 I looked at contained this food colouring.
Carminic acid E120	See *carmines* and *cochineal*.	
Carmoisine E122	This is an artificial *azo dye* food colouring. It is used to give foods a red colour. It is also called *azorubine*.	This is one of five food colourants that the Food Standards Agency in the UK is currently recommending should be avoided if your child shows symptoms of hyperactivity. For more information see Chapter 2 (Colourings).
		This is one of the food additives currently under review by the European Food Safety Authority. This may lead to a change in regulation sometime in 2008. For updated information about this food dye see the website www.whatsinthis.co.uk.
		I found it in 7 out of the 570 products I looked at and these

INGREDIENT	WHAT IS IT?	FURTHER INFORMATION
		were yogurts and yogurt drinks, brightly coloured confectionery, cake decorations, cake mixes and jelly.
Carnauba wax E903	This is a wax that comes from a Brazilian palm tree. It is used as a *glazing agent* to give a shiny attractive appearance and as a coating that helps to reduce moisture loss.	
Carob bean gum E410	Also known as *locust bean gum*. This is a gum extracted from the seeds of the carob tree. It is used as an *emulsifier* and *stabiliser* in foods.	I found this in many children's yogurts. This is an additive permitted in organic foods. For more information about organic foods see Chapter 2 and Appendix 2.
Carrageenan E407	This is a naturally occurring carbohydrate (sugar) derived from a variety of red seaweed. The seaweed is boiled to extract the carrageenan. It is used for its *thickening*, *gelling* and *stabilising* properties.	This is an additive permitted in organic foods. For more information about organic foods see Chapter 2 and Chapter 7.
Carrot	This is an orange-coloured root vegetable.	It is a rich source of *vitamin A* and contains some *dietary fibre*.
Carrot concentrate	This is the same as *carrot powder*.	
Carrot powder	This is usually produced by freeze-drying fresh carrots and then grinding them into a powder.	
Cashew nuts	This nut is the fruit of a tree.	Cashew nuts are a source of protein, *niacin*, *zinc* and *iron*. They are a source of monounsaturated *fat*.

INGREDIENT	WHAT IS IT?	FURTHER INFORMATION
Caustic sulphite caramel E150b	This is one of four caramel colourants used by food manufacturers, ranging from light brown to very dark brown in colour. They are produced by heating carbohydrates (e.g. sugars or malt syrups) in the presence of small amounts of food-grade acids, alkalis or salts.	Research into this food colourant and a link to asthma and skin irritation has not been scientifically conclusive. However, this is one of the food colours the Children's Hyperactivity Support Group recommends is avoided by sensitive children.
	These colours are the most commonly used colourants in food.	I found this food colour in just over 60% of the products I looked at which contained food colours.
	Caramel is also used in *flavourings*.	
Cayenne	This is a hot red chilli from the pepper family. It is sometimes used in a dried and ground powder form to add flavour to foods.	
Celery extract	This is when the oil is extracted from celery, which is very concentrated in celery flavour. It is used to flavour foods and is often found in stocks.	
Celery flavouring	This is a flavouring that has been created using real celery or has been recreated in a laboratory to be so similar to real celery that it can be called celery flavouring.	
Cellulose gum E460	This is derived from cellulose, which is the main component in green plants. It is used as a *stabiliser*, *thickener* and *bulking agent* in foods.	There is little digestion of cellulose in the human digestive tract but it serves the purpose of bulking waste and is part of what is known as *dietary fibre*.

INGREDIENT	WHAT IS IT?	FURTHER INFORMATION
Cheese	Cheese is made by separating the solid component of milk (curd) from the liquid part (*whey*). It is made mainly from cows' milk but can also be made from sheep, goat and buffalo milk. Cheeses other than cottage cheese and cream cheeses are cured by being left to mature with salt under various conditions that produce the characteristic flavours of each type of cheese. When 'cheese' is on the ingredients list it means natural cheese has been used. See also *processed cheese*.	Cheeses differ in fat and water contents. They retain much of the calcium from the milk and many contain a relatively high amount of sodium (salt). All cheeses are a good source of calcium. They are also a source of protein. Much of the *fat* content is saturated.
Cheese powder	This is *cheese* which has had the water content removed and then been ground to a powder. Sometimes it may be part cheese and part milk powder – this should be stated clearly.	
Cherry extracts	See *fruit extracts*.	
Chestnut flour	Chestnuts are the fruits of the chestnut tree (a beech tree family member). This is not the same as water chestnuts. Chestnuts can be candied (*marrons glacés*) or roasted or added to cakes and breads as a flour.	
Chicken	This is a type of meat.	Chicken meat is a rich source of protein and *niacin*, a good source of selenium and a

INGREDIENT	WHAT IS IT?	FURTHER INFORMATION
		source of *iron* and *vitamin B1*, vitamin B2 and *vitamin B6*. Breast meat is lower in *fat* than darker thigh or leg meat. About 30% of the fat is saturated.
Chicken extract	This is dried *chicken* meat that has been ground to a powder.	
Chicken fat	This is when just the fat from *chicken* meat has been extracted and used on its own in a product. This can help to give a stronger chicken flavour and boost the texture or 'mouth feel' of a product.	
Chickpea	These are mild-flavoured beans and classed as a pulse. They are used puréed in dips such as hummus and are also sometimes used ground into a flour (gram flour) and used in Indian and Middle Eastern cooking.	Chickpeas are a good source of *folate*, a source of protein, *vitamin A* and *iron*. They are low in *fat* and provide some *dietary fibre*.
Chilli pepper	This is the name for a small, hotter version of the large red peppers. They add flavour to food.	
Chives	This is a herb that is part of the onion family and has a mild onion flavour. Chives are used to add natural flavour to foods.	
Chocolate	This is made from cocoa beans by processing them and adding sugar, *cocoa butter* (or sometimes vegetable oils	Milk chocolate is a source of calcium, protein, *iron* and vitamin B2. It contains 30% *fat* of which 60% is saturated.

INGREDIENT	WHAT IS IT?	FURTHER INFORMATION
	instead), usually *flavourings* are added, *lecithin* and, if milk chocolate, then *milk solids* are added.	Chocolate can also be high in added sugar, which adds to the calories as well as not being healthy for teeth.
Chocolate chips	These are usually made of *chocolate* that has been broken into small chunks. There will be a breakdown of what ingredients are in the chips somewhere on the label.	
Chocolate flavour coating	When a product uses the term 'chocolate flavour' it means that an artificial chocolate flavouring has been used, which does not have to contain any actual chocolate. 'Chocolate flavoured' means that the coating contains some real chocolate.	
Cider vinegar	A vinegar produced from apples.	
Cinnamon	Ground powder form of a tree bark; it has a distinctive flavour and is used in many savoury and sweet foods.	
Citric acid E330	This is a weak acid found naturally in citrus fruits. It is used as a natural *preservative*, to add sharp acidic flavour to food and drinks and is also antimicrobial. Food manufacturers produce it by fermenting sucrose with a natural fungus.	It is very widely used. This additive is permitted in organic foods. For more information about organic foods see Chapter 2 and Appendix 2.

INGREDIENT	WHAT IS IT?	FURTHER INFORMATION
Clove (extract)	These are unopened flower buds of the clove tree; when dried they are used in cooking to add flavour to foods. Manufacturers sometimes add clove extract, i.e. oil from crushed cloves, in a product to add flavour.	
Cochineal E120	This is a natural food colour derived from cochineal (an insect). It is a deep red colour. Also listed under *carmines* and *carminic acid* on a food label.	10 products out of 570 I looked at contained this food colouring.
Cocoa butter	This is the fat from the cocoa bean. It is produced by pressing or by solvent extraction of ground roasted cocoa beans, and is used in the making of chocolate.	
Cocoa liquor	Finely ground cocoa beans turn into a thick liquid when heated and this is known as cocoa liquor.	
Cocoa mass	This is what is left after the cocoa beans have been roasted and ground to a paste. It is made up of cocoa powder / cocoa solids and cocoa butter.	
Cocoa powder	Made from the cocoa bean, which is pulped and then the cocoa butter is removed to leave cocoa powder. It is used as a natural colouring and flavouring in chocolate foods and drinks.	Cocoa powder is low in *fat* and is not a high source of *sugar*.
Cocoa solids	This is another term for cocoa powder. It contains no *sugar*,	

INGREDIENT	WHAT IS IT?	FURTHER INFORMATION
	just pure cocoa powder. Dark chocolate is usually over 50% cocoa solids, milk chocolate around 30% and white chocolate contains no cocoa solids or powder, just cocoa butter.	
Coconut	This is the fruit of a tropical palm tree.	
Coconut oil	This is the natural oil from the *coconut* fruit.	It is 90% saturated *fat* so is best kept to a minimum in children's diets.
Cod	This is a white fish.	This is a good source of *protein* and low in *fat*.
Comminuted lemon from concentrate	Comminute means that the whole fruit (without the skin) has been pulverised rather than just the juice being extracted. This means that some of the pith and fibre in the lemon is found in the product. Concentrate means that the pulverised fruit product has then had the water removed i.e. dehydrated. So this term basically means dehydrated pulverised lemon.	
Concentrated apple purée	See *concentrated fruit purée*.	
Concentrated butter	*Butter* is melted and then processed to increase the fat content to 96% or more; this is called concentrated butter. The higher *fat* content makes it more stable for use in foods than normal butter.	

INGREDIENT	WHAT IS IT?	FURTHER INFORMATION
Concentrated fruit purée	This is when puréed fruit has had some or all of the water content removed and it becomes very concentrated in flavour and fruit sugar.	
Concentrated lemon juice	This is when lemon juice has had some of the water removed from it to create a more concentrated substance. Can be used to add flavour to foods or as an *antioxidant* and *preservative*, i.e. to stop food or drink discolouring.	
Concentrated skimmed milk	This is created by removing the fat from whole milk (to make it skimmed) and then removing some of the water content to produce a concentrated *milk solids* product.	
Concentrated strawberry purée	See *concentrated fruit purée*.	
Concentrated tomato purée	This is when *tomato purée* has some of its water content removed to make it more intense as a flavour.	
Concentrated whey	*Whey* is a liquid formed from milk left over when you make cheese. It is used as an ingredient in some foods as it contains about 1% protein, all the milk lactose and some vitamins and minerals, so it has some nutritional value. It is 92% water. By removing some of the water then the whey becomes concentrated.	

INGREDIENT	WHAT IS IT?	FURTHER INFORMATION
Condensed milk	This is milk which has had some of the water evaporated from it to create a thicker substance. It is usually sold in tins and has been sweetened with added sugar. It is used as an ingredient in puddings, confectionery and pies.	
Copper complexes of chlorophyllins E141	This is a natural food colouring derived from chlorophyll, the natural green pigment in plants. It gives food a green colour.	I found this in 4 products out of the 570 I looked at and these were all sweets and confectionery.
Coriander leaf	Coriander is a green leaf herb, used to add flavour to foods.	
Corn	This is a grain also known as *maize*. Corn is processed into a large number of products including corn oil, corn syrup, *corn flour, corn starch* and cornflakes. It has no *gluten*, so is also used as a flour in making gluten-free breads and pastas. The flowering part of corn develops into corn kernels, otherwise known as corn on the cob. The kernels can be eaten as an unprocessed vegetable, i.e. sweet corn, as well as used to make popcorn.	It is not as nutritionally rich as other grains because it is lower in some proteins. When processed in the form in which it is most commonly used in foods then it does not contain significant amounts of fibre, vitamins and minerals. Sweet corn is a source of *vitamin C* and provides some *dietary fibre*. Cornflakes as a breakfast cereal are usually enriched with vitamins and minerals.
Corn dextrose	*Dextrose* is an alternative name for *glucose*. Commercially the term glucose is used to mean *corn syrup* (a mixture of	

	glucose, sugars and dextrins) and pure *glucose* is called *dextrose*. Commonly used to sweeten foods.	
Corn flour	Corn flour is made from milled corn grains. It is also called *corn starch*. It is commonly used as a *thickener* in foods, e.g. custard, sauces and gravies.	
Corn starch	This is another name for *corn flour*.	
Corn syrup	This is a sweetener manufactured from *corn starch*. It is used as a sweetener as well as a *thickener* and *humectant*.	
Cotto ham	This means cooked ham in Italian. This is often listed as an ingredient in pasta and pizza dishes using ham.	
Cottonseed oil	This is a pale-yellow vegetable oil extracted from the cotton plant seed.	The oil is 25% saturated and 50% polyunsaturated.
Cream cheese	Cheese is made by separating the solid component of milk (curd) from the liquid part (*whey*). Cream cheese is a mild cheese that is a mixture of *cream* and *milk*. It is different from other cheeses as it is eaten fresh i.e. not matured like other soft cheeses and hard cheeses. It contains a minimum of 33% fat unless stated as a lower-fat version.	The full-fat version of cream cheese usually just contains cheese, whereas the reduced-fat versions will have other added ingredients, which replace the taste and texture that the fat would provide.

INGREDIENT	WHAT IS IT?	FURTHER INFORMATION
Cream of tartar E336	This is another word for *potassium tartrates* and is commonly used as a *raising agent* in foods.	
Cream powder	This is when *cream* has had the water content removed and then been ground to a powder.	
Crème fraîche	This is *cream* that has been slightly soured by adding bacteria to give it a mildly sour flavour. Not as sour or as thick as sour cream.	
Crisped rice / crispy rice	This is another word for puffed *rice*, when rice grains are heated under pressure until they explode.	
Crushed whole fruit	This is when whole fruit is mechanically squashed to a purée-like consistency.	
Cumin	This is a spice from a plant and has a distinctive flavour used in Indian cuisine.	
Curcumin E100	This is a natural food colouring made from the pigment of the spice *turmeric*. It gives foods a yellow colour.	Curcumin is also a powerful natural *antioxidant* so may have health benefits. I found it in 10 out of 570 products, including sweets and cake mixes.
Curry powder	This is a mix of several spices that have been ground to a powder form. Commonly used to flavour Indian-style dishes and sauces.	

INGREDIENT	WHAT IS IT?	FURTHER INFORMATION
Dates	These are grown on trees and usually eaten in their dried form. Dried dates are also used in cereal bars, cake baking and muesli.	Dried dates provide a concentrated source of *sucrose* (up to 60%), i.e. sugar. They also supply some *dietary fibre*.
Dehydrated potato	This is another term for dried *potato*, i.e. when the moisture/water is removed through drying.	
Delta tocopherol E309	This is a synthetic version of *vitamin E*. It is used as an *antioxidant*. It is no different to natural sources of *vitamin E* in the body.	
Demerara sugar	This is a pale-coloured and mild-flavoured *cane sugar* with large golden crystals, which is grown in Guyana. It is the stage before pure white sugar in processing.	Nutritionally it contains only slightly less *sucrose*, i.e. sugar. Fully refined white sugar is 100% *sucrose*.
Demineralised whey powder	This is *whey powder* which has had most (70–90%) of the natural minerals (e.g. calcium) removed.	
Desiccated coconut	Desiccation is an alternative term for drying. This is dried and shredded coconut. It is usually sweetened for use in	

INGREDIENT	WHAT IS IT?	FURTHER INFORMATION
	foods. The unsweetened variety may be used in muesli.	
Dextrin	This is the name for mixtures of soluble compounds formed by the partial breakdown of *starch (carbohydrate)* by heat, acid or enzymes. It is used for a variety of functions including as a *thickener*, to prevent crystallisation and as a gum.	Nutritionally equivalent to *starch (carbohydrate)*.
Dextrose	This is an alternative name for *glucose* (derived from *corn*). Commonly used as a sweetener in foods, it is about 70% as sweet as *sucrose*.	It is rapidly absorbed and digested which means it has a high *glycaemic index* (GI). For more information about GI see Chapter 2.
Dextrose monohydrate	This is also known as *glucose*. It is used to sweeten foods.	
Dietary Fibre	This is a type of *carbohydrate* which is found in plant cell walls. It is important for a healthy digestive system by helping regular bowel movements. It is found in fruit, vegetables, wholegrains e.g. oats, brown rice, wholemeal flour.	For more information see Chapter 3: What Every Parent Should Know About Children's Nutrition.
Dill	A herb used to flavour foods. Especially popular in sauces to accompany fish.	
Dimethyl dicarbonate E242	This is used as a *preservative* and also a sterilant in foods and wines.	

INGREDIENT	WHAT IS IT?	FURTHER INFORMATION
Diphosphates E450	Made synthetically and used for its ability as a *gelling agent*, *emulsifier* and *stabiliser*.	I found it most commonly used in cheese products.
Disodium 5'-riboneucleotides E635	This is a synthetically made *flavour enhancer*.	I found this used in a few varieties of crisps.
Disodium dihydrogen diphosphate E450a	Made synthetically and used for its ability as a *gelling agent*, *emulsifier* and *stabiliser*.	
Disodium guanylate E627	Often used in combination with *monosodium glutamate (MSG)* this is a synthetically made *flavour enhancer*.	I found this used in crisps, cured meat products and packet noodle meals.
Disodium phosphate E450c	Made synthetically and used for its ability as a *gelling agent*, *emulsifier* and *stabiliser*.	
Double cream	This is *cream* with a minimum fat content of 48%.	
Dried apple	See *dried fruit*.	
Dried apricot	See *dried fruit*.	
Dried egg white	Egg white which has had the water content removed so it becomes a powder; it has a long shelf life.	
Dried fruit	Dried fruits are when fresh fruit has been dried either naturally or in a machine until much of the water content has evaporated. Dried fruit has a long shelf life.	Dried fruit is a source of dietary fibre. Remember, it is also easier to eat, say, 4 dried apricots than 4 fresh ones, so more sugar may be consumed.

INGREDIENT	WHAT IS IT?	FURTHER INFORMATION
	Sweetness and flavour are concentrated by the drying process but nutrients, especially vitamins, can be lost e.g. *vitamin C* and *A*. The drying process means dried fruit is lower in *fructose* and higher in *sucrose* than fresh fruit.	The colour of the fruit is often preserved during the drying process by spraying it with *sulphur dioxide* (E220). Sulphur dioxide may trigger asthma in sensitive individuals. For more information about sulphur dioxide see Chapter 2 ('Preservatives').
Dried glucose syrup	This is *glucose syrup* which has had some or all of the water content removed so it becomes a powder.	
Dried malt extract	*Malt* is derived from maltose (which is a sugar found in grains such as barley or wheat). It can be dehydrated. It is used as a *flavouring*.	
Dried onion	Onion which has been dehydrated, i.e. the water content removed. Used to add flavour.	
Dried parsley	Parsley is a green leaf herb used to add flavour to foods. It can be freeze-dried, i.e. the water is removed.	
Dried pear	See *dried fruit*.	
Dried porcini mushrooms	Porcini mushrooms are a type of mushroom with a meaty texture and a strong taste. They are often found in the dried form, i.e. they have had the water content removed.	

INGREDIENT	WHAT IS IT?	FURTHER INFORMATION
Dried skimmed milk	Skimmed milk which has had the water content removed so it becomes a powder. It has a long shelf life.	
Dried tomato	Fresh tomato which has been dehydrated i.e. the water content reduced. This provides flavour and colour to foods.	
Dried wheat gluten	*Gluten* is a protein found in the wheat grain. It is sometimes used separately from wheat as it has binding properties.	
Dried whey	*Whey* is a liquid formed from milk, left over when you make *cheese*. It is used as an ingredient in some foods as it contains about 1% protein, all the milk lactose and some vitamins and minerals, so it has some nutritional value. It is 92% water. By removing some of the water then the whey becomes concentrated.	
Dried whole milk	Another name for powdered whole milk.	
Dried yogurt	This is when yogurt has had the water content removed so it becomes dehydrated and a powder form. This gives it a longer shelf life.	
Dry molasses	This is when *molasses* (a thick syrup by-product of sugar processing) is dehydrated, i.e. has the water removed so it becomes a powder form. It can	

INGREDIENT	WHAT IS IT?	FURTHER INFORMATION
	add flavour and sweetness to foods.	
Durum Wheat	This is the type of wheat grain which is used to make pasta and some breads, because it has a higher protein and *gluten* content than other forms of wheat.	
Durum wheat semolina	This is part of the *durum wheat* grain and is often used in pastas and breads.	

INGREDIENT	WHAT IS IT?	FURTHER INFORMATION
Edamer cheese	This is the Dutch word for Edam cheese.	
Edible starches	This is when *starch* (*carbohydrate*) has been used in the product derived from any (non-specific) grain source. 'Edible' means can be eaten.	
Eggs	These are used in food preparation, e.g. cake baking and meringues, and they help to thicken sauces and are a great binding agent.	Eggs are a source of *vitamin D* and *vitamin B12*, *protein*, *niacin*, *vitamin A*, vitamin B2 and *zinc*. They are about 13% *fat* of which 35% is saturated and 50% is mono-unsaturated. Most of the fat is found in the egg yolk.
Egg albumen	This is another word for egg white.	
Egg pasta	Pasta made from *durum wheat* with some whole egg added to help texture.	
Egg powder	This is when whole egg has had the water content removed to form a dry powder. This has a long shelf life.	
Elderberry	This is a berry fruit.	It is high in *vitamin C* and *antioxidants*.

INGREDIENT	WHAT IS IT?	FURTHER INFORMATION
Emmental cheese	This is a Swiss cheese with large holes.	
Emulsifier	These are substances which are used to help ingredients blend together when processed or cooked, in particular to help oils and water mix together. These are listed on ingredients lists with their specific name.	*Lecithin* is a very commonly used one.
Emulsifying salts E127	These are substances which are added to foods to keep them stable and keep them firm and 'together'. They are listed on ingredients lists with their specific name.	I found these commonly used in cheeses and cheese products.
Erythrosine E127	This is an artificial food colouring. It gives a red colour. Often used to add the colour back to glacé cherries lost during processing.	I found it in 3 products, which all contained glacé cherries. No supposed links to asthma, hyperactivity, allergic reactions and skin reactions have been scientifically proven. However, it is one of the food colours recommended by the Children's Hyperactivity Support Group be avoided in diets of sensitive children.
Essential fats/ essential fatty acids (EFA)	This term refers to a group of important *fats* which the body cannot make itself so it needs to get them from food. These essential polyunsaturated fats are known as *omega 3* and *omega 6* fats.	For more information about *fats* see Chapter 3.

INGREDIENT	WHAT IS IT?	FURTHER INFORMATION
Ethyl p-hydroxyben-zoate E214	This is one of the group of *preservatives* called benzoates which are derived from benzoic acid.	I found this in 5 out of 7 children's medicines I looked at. The Food Standards Agency currently advise that benzoates could make symptoms of asthma and eczema worse in children with these conditions. For more information on the Benzoates see Chapter 2 ('Preservatives').
Extra-virgin olive oil	This refers to the oil produced from crushing olives mechanically or physically. This method produces the highest quality *olive oil*. It has not been chemically treated in any way.	

INGREDIENT	WHAT IS IT?	FURTHER INFORMATION
Fat	This is a nutrient found in foods. It provides 9 calories per gram. There are two types of natural fats found in foods: saturated (animal origin) and unsaturated (vegetable origin).	For more information about Fats see Chapter 3: What Every Parent Should Know About Children's Nutrition.
Fat-enriched skimmed milk powder	This is basically skimmed milk powder, i.e. dried skimmed milk which has had some fat added, often a vegetable fat.	
Fat-reduced cocoa powder	*Cocoa powder* which has had most of the fat content removed.	
Fatty acids	Fat is made up of different types of fatty acids, e.g. saturated fatty acids and unsaturated fatty acids which include *essential fatty acids*, polyunsaturated fatty acids and mono-unsaturated fatty acids. Fatty acids occur naturally and are derived from animal fats, fish oils and vegetable fats. They are used in foods as *emulsifiers* and *stabilisers*.	
Fennel seeds	These are the seeds from the fennel plant and they have a slight liquorice flavour. They are used to add flavour to foods.	

INGREDIENT	WHAT IS IT?	FURTHER INFORMATION
Fermented wheat flour	This is when the wheat grain has been treated with *yeast* or bacteria to change the *sugar* or *carbohydrate* content into an acid or alcohol. Fermentation is used to add fullness of flavour and improve preservation.	
Fermented wheat starch	This is when the *carbohydrate* or *starch* in the wheat grain has been treated with bacteria or *yeast* to change it to an acid or alcohol. Fermentation is used to add fullness of flavour and improve preservation.	
Ferrous sulphate	This is a salt of the naturally occurring mineral *iron*. It is the form of iron used to fortify foods.	
Figs	These are a fruit which can be eaten fresh or dried.	Figs have a mild laxative effect. They are a source of calcium, *iron* and *dietary fibre*.
Firming agent	These are used to retain firmness and crispness in products even when they are processed. Many foods contain natural firming agents, e.g. *pectin* in apples.	
Fish gelatin(e)	This is extracted from the skin of fish. It is used to protect against moisture loss and so can help to preserve a food.	
Flavour	When something is referred to as 'flavour', e.g. raspberry flavour, it means that an artificial flavouring has been	By knowing the difference between the legal definitions of 'flavour' and 'flavoured' parents will be able to make informed

122

INGREDIENT	WHAT IS IT?	FURTHER INFORMATION
	used rather than any actual raspberries.	choices about products where these terms are used.
Flavoured	When something is referred to as being 'flavoured' with something, e.g. raspberry flavoured, then legally it must contain some of that ingredient (in this case real raspberries).	By knowing the difference between the legal definitions of 'flavour' and 'flavoured' parents will be able to make informed choices about products where these terms are used.
Flavour enhancers	These help perk up the flavour of a product. They do not have any characteristic flavour of their own but added to foods they act to enhance the flavour of that food. Salt is the most widely used flavour enhancer, though it is not classed as an additive.	_Monosodium glutamate_ (MSG) is a commonly used one.
Flavourings	These are substances used to give flavour and/or smell to a product. There are natural ones, nature-identical ones, synthetic (man-made) ones and smoke flavourings. The specific flavouring used in a product does not have to be listed under current EU legislation. There are over 2,500 flavourings currently permitted in food use.	Under EU legislation the expression 'Natural Flavourings' can only be used on those extracted from vegetable or animal materials. Where the term 'Flavourings' is used then these will be artificial.
Flour treatment agents	These help to keep white flour white and make a flour less 'strong' and so more suitable for cake baking than bread making. The specific names will be listed on the ingredients list.	

INGREDIENT	WHAT IS IT?	FURTHER INFORMATION
Folate	See *Folic acid*.	
Folic acid	This is one of the B vitamins. It is important for the production of new cells. It is found naturally in foods such as green leafy vegetables, whole grains and pulses. It is also added to many breads and breakfast cereals.	For the Recommended Daily Amounts (RDA) of this nutrient see page 16.
Fondant icing	This is a mixture of *sugar syrup* and *glucose* mixed together and heated to create a smooth paste used in foods or to decorate foods.	
Formed smoked ham	The term 'formed' means that the pork meat is not cut from a whole piece of meat but formed using bits of pork meat. *Smoking* is a process of flavouring, preserving or cooking foods.	
Free range	This term means that the animals or the animals who produced the products, e.g. dairy or eggs, have been kept in certain specified conditions, e.g. allowed to spend time outside roaming freely over land, a maximum number of animals kept per hectare, etc.	This term is used for meats, poultry and eggs. The legal definitions differ for different animals.
Freeze dried	This is a method of preservation and involves foods being rapidly frozen and then placed in a vacuum. This is used as a way of dehydrating foods, which can lengthen the shelf life and reduce their weight.	

INGREDIENT	WHAT IS IT?	FURTHER INFORMATION
Fromage frais	This is a soft unmatured fresh *cheese*. It is 80% water and is made from skimmed or semi-skimmed milk.	It is a rich source of *vitamin B12*, a good source of vitamin B2 and a source of protein and *vitamin A*. It also contains calcium and is about 8% *fat*.
Fructo-oligosac-charide	This is a natural plant sugar which has a sweet taste but, as it cannot be fully digested by the body, it does not cause a rise in blood-sugar levels and has a reduced calorific value. It is used as a sweetener in foods as well as a way of adding fibre.	It is a rich source of *dietary fibre*. It is not harmful to teeth and is also a *prebiotic*. For more information about prebiotics see Chapter 2 (What Are Functional Foods?).
Fructose	Also known as fruit sugar, this is a sugar found naturally occurring in fruits and root vegetables, e.g. beetroot, parsnips, sweet potatoes. It is 1.7 times sweeter to taste than *sucrose* (table sugar).	As the fruit sugars have been extracted out of the whole fruits they are no longer in combination with fibre and water. Fructose has a high *Glycaemic Index* (GI) which means it is quickly digested and absorbed into the blood. Fructose is not harmful to teeth in the same way as sucrose.
Fructose-dextrose syrup	This is another name for the more commonly used *Fructose-glucose syrup*.	
Fructose-glucose syrup	This is a sweet syrup which is 40–90% *fructose* and is made from *glucose syrup* (from *corn*). It is used as a sweetener in foods. See also *glucose-fructose syrup*.	
Fruit extracts	These are preparations obtained from fruits by various means. They may also be made	

INGREDIENT	WHAT IS IT?	FURTHER INFORMATION
	synthetically but are nature identical. These are used as natural flavourings.	
Fruit juice from concentrate	These are fruit juices which have been concentrated by evaporation or freezing to remove the water contents of them. This is often done so that the weight of them is less when transporting them long distances, often across the world. The water is then added back into them in the UK either by the manufacturer (fruit juices) or by the consumer (squashes and cordial drinks).	Sometimes fruit concentrates are used in their concentrated form in foods such as juices, smoothies and yogurts to add extra sweetness to the product. These are commonly apple and grape concentrates. For more information about the nutritional value of fruit juices see Chapter 3.
Fruit purée	Fruit flesh which is blended to a soft thick liquid.	Used in many fruit juices, fruit smoothies and yogurts.
Fruit purée from concentrate	Fruit purée which has been concentrated by evaporation or freezing to remove the water content. This is often done so that the weight of them is less when transporting them long distances, often across the world.	Used in fruit yogurts, smoothies and puddings.
Fruit sugar	Also known as *fructose* and is a sugar found naturally occurring in fruits and root vegetables, e.g. beetroot, parsnips, sweet potatoes. It is 1.7 times sweeter to taste than *sucrose* (table sugar).	As the fruit sugars have been extracted out of the whole fruits they are no longer in combination with fibre and water. Fructose has a high *Glycaemic Index* (GI) which means it is quickly digested and absorbed into the blood. Fructose is not harmful to teeth in the same way as *sucrose*.

INGREDIENT	WHAT IS IT?	FURTHER INFORMATION
Full cream milk	Another name for whole milk.	
Full cream milk powder	Another term for *dried whole milk*, i.e. the water content has been removed from whole milk to produce a powder. This extends the shelf life and reduces the weight of it in products.	
Fumaric Acid E297	This is a natural organic acid which is used as a flavouring. It also helps foods to rise and has an *antioxidant* effect. Found in packet desserts and baked goods.	

INGREDIENT	WHAT IS IT?	FURTHER INFORMATION
Galacto-oligosaccharides	This is a natural *prebiotic* and is sometimes added to yogurts as a functional food or to add some sweetness to foods (they are more stable when heated than *sucrose*).	These are present naturally in breast milk. For more information about functional foods and prebiotics see Chapter 2.
Gamma tocopherol E308	A synthetic version of *vitamin E*. It is used as an *antioxidant*. It is not seen differently by the body than natural sources of vitamin E.	
Garam masala	This is a blend of spices in powder form which is used to add flavour to Indian-style dishes and sauces. It can contain up to 12 different spices and literally means 'warm spice'.	
Gardenia	This is a flower which can sometimes be used as a natural flavouring.	
Garlic powder	This is when garlic has been dehydrated, i.e. the water content is removed and then it is ground to a powder. It is used as a natural flavouring in foods.	
Garlic purée	Fresh garlic which has been puréed.	

INGREDIENT	WHAT IS IT?	FURTHER INFORMATION
Garlic salt	Usually garlic which has been dehydrated to form a powder and then has some salt added. Used to add flavour to foods.	
Gelatine E441	This is a soluble protein prepared from collagen (a component found in animal skin) or bones by boiling with water. It is used as a *gelling agent* in sugar confectionery, jellies, ice cream, yogurt, fresh fruit cakes and in tinned meats. It is also used in the pharmaceutical industry in capsules.	
Gellan gum E418	This is a complex *carbohydrate* produced by fermentation. It is used as a *gelling agent*.	
Gelling agent	Used in foods for their capability to form a jelly. Usually derived from natural sources, e.g. seaweed, apples, gum trees. The exact one used is specified on the label.	
Ginger	This is a root of a tropical plant which is used to flavour foods. It has a spicy pungent flavour and is common is Indian and Asian cuisines. It can be used in a fresh raw form or powder form and can also be used in sweet dishes; raw ginger slices are eaten with Japanese foods such as sushi.	

INGREDIENT	WHAT IS IT?	FURTHER INFORMATION
Glacé cherries	Glacé cherries are made by heating the cherries in a *sugar syrup*.	They tend to lose their colour when processed so a red food colouring (*Erythrosine* E127) is commonly added.
Glazing agent	A substance used to provide a shiny appearance or protective coating to foods.	
Glucono-delta-lactone E575	This is derived from *glucose* and is used as a sequestrant.	
Glucose	Glucose is the main energy source for living cells. *Carbohydrate* foods are digested down into glucose in the body. Glucose is a natural *sugar* found in honey and fruits and is also found in *sucrose* (table sugar). It can be commercially manufactured by the hydrolysis of starches such as *corn*. Hydrolysis is when a nutrient is split into its different components by the action of water using catalysts such as enzymes, acids or alkalis.	
Glucose syrup	This is a syrup consisting predominantly of *glucose* and produced commercially mainly from *corn*. This is added to foods for sweetness or texture.	This has a high *Glycaemic Index* (GI), which means it is digested and absorbed into the blood quickly. For more information about GI see Chapter 2.
Glucose-fructose syrup	This is a sweet syrup made from *glucose syrup* (from *corn*) and contains some *fructose*.	

INGREDIENT	WHAT IS IT?	FURTHER INFORMATION
	It is used as a sweetener in foods. It is sweeter than *fructose-glucose syrup* as it has a higher glucose content.	
Glutamic acid	Glutamic acid is a naturally occurring amino acid (protein) which is found in virtually all protein-containing foods and is manufactured by the body and is present in breast milk.	The *flavour enhancer monosodium glutamate* is the sodium salt of glutamic acid.
Gluten	This is a protein which is found in four grains: wheat, oats, rye and barley. It is a binding protein and is sometimes extracted from the grain and used as an ingredient in foods because of this binding ability.	The majority of the population have no problem digesting gluten. However, for some people gluten can be damaging to their digestive system and this condition is known as coeliac disease.
Gluten-free wheat fibre	This appears on an ingredients list when just a high-fibre part of the wheat grain has been added to the product. The fibre contains no *gluten*.	
Glycaemic Index (GI)	GI is a ranking system for *carbohydrate*-containing foods based on their effect on blood sugar (*glucose*) levels. GI runs from 0—100 and usually uses glucose (which has a GI value of 100) as a reference point. The effect other foods have on blood sugar levels are then compared to this.	For more information about Carbohydrates see Chapter 3: What Every Parent Should Know About Children's Nutrition. For more about GI see Chapter 2.
Glycerin	This is another word for *glycerol*.	

INGREDIENT	WHAT IS IT?	FURTHER INFORMATION
Glycerol E422	This is a clear odourless sweet-tasting liquid derived from fats. Used as a *humectant* in foods, i.e. to stop them drying out. It is also used to improve texture in cakes and to dissolve flavourings.	This additive is permitted in organic foods. For more information about organic foods see Chapter 2 and Appendix 2.
Goats' cheese	A *cheese* made from goats' milk.	
Golden syrup	This is a light-coloured syrup made by the evaporation of *cane sugar* juice.	
Granulated sugar	This is made from the crystallisation of *sugar syrup* and is the most pure (processed) form of sugar manufactured from sugar cane and sugar beet.	Contains at least 98.8% *sucrose*. It has no nutritional value other than a sugar and contains no vitamins, minerals, protein or *dietary fibre*.
Green bell pepper	A type of *bell pepper*.	
Green S E142	This is an artificial food colouring. It gives a green colour to food.	I found it in 2 products: a cake mix and a cordial drink. No supposed links to asthma, hyperactivity, allergic reactions and skin reactions have been scientifically proven. However, it is one of the food colours recommended by the Children's Hyperactivity Support Group be avoided in diets of sensitive children.
Ground paprika E160c	*Paprika* is a natural food colouring made from the pigment of red *bell pepper*. It is	I found it used in savoury products, crisps, ready-meals and sweets.

INGREDIENT	WHAT IS IT?	FURTHER INFORMATION
	dried and then ground to form a powder. It is also used as a natural flavouring.	
Guar gum E412	This is a gum obtained from the seeds of a tree. It is used as a *stabiliser*, *thickener* and *emulsifier* in foods such as yogurts. It is also common in slimming or reduced-fat products, as it is not digested by the body.	I found this in many yogurts. This is one of the additives permitted in organic foods. For more information about organic foods see Chapter 2 and Appendix 2.
Gum arabic E414	This is a type of gum extracted from the African acacia tree. It can also be known as *acacia gum*. It has many uses including a *thickener*, *stabiliser*, *emulsifier* and *glazing agent*, and can also help stop *sugar* from crystallising.	Research studies in humans looking at the suggested links between *acacia gum* and asthma and skin irritability have not been conclusive. This additive is one permitted in organic foods. For more information about organic foods see Chapter 2 and Appendix 2.
Gum base	This is the ingredient in chewing gum that allows it to be chewed over and over again. It used to be made from natural resins but these have become more scarce, so it is now made synthetically.	
Gum tragacanth E413	This is a natural plant gum and is used as a *stabiliser*, *thickener* and to add texture to foods.	

INGREDIENT	WHAT IS IT?	FURTHER INFORMATION
Hardened vegetable fat	This is another name for *hydrogenated vegetable fat*.	
Haricot beans	These are small white beans. The mature beans are used in baked beans.	Haricot beans are a source of protein, *vitamin B1*, *iron* and *dietary fibre*. They are very low in *fat*.
Hazelnuts	Grown on a tree. They are sometimes added to desserts, cakes, muesli and cereal bars.	Hazelnuts are a rich source of *vitamin E*, a source of protein, *niacin*, *vitamin B1* and vitamin B2, calcium, *zinc* and *iron*. They contain about 32% *fat* (most of which is mono-unsaturated).
Herb extract	This is where the essential oils of a mix of herbs have been extracted. This is used as a natural flavouring.	
High fructose corn syrup	This is the same as *Fructose-glucose syrup*. This is a sweet syrup which is 40–90% *fructose* and is made from *glucose syrup* (from *corn*). It is used as a sweetener in foods. See also *Glucose-fructose syrup*.	
Honey	A sweet natural liquid produced by bees from flower nectar.	As it is rich in fructose and glucose it is digested and absorbed by the blood quickly. It

INGREDIENT	WHAT IS IT?	FURTHER INFORMATION
	It is about 80% sugars (mainly *fructose* and *glucose*) and 20% water.	has a high *Glycaemic Index* (GI). For more information about GI see Chapter 2.
		It does contain some vitamins and minerals, which table sugar does not, and may also have other properties such as antibacterial or healing ones.
Horseradish powder	Horseradish is a tree root which is used to flavour foods. It is a main component in horseradish sauce (popular with roast meats) and also in the Japanese condiment wasabi.	
Humectant	These help to increase or maintain the moisture contents of foods. This helps to stop the growth of mould or stop a food drying out.	
Hydrogenated soya oil	This is when soya oil (derived from soya beans) has been chemically processed to make it harder, i.e. solid at room temperature. This means it lasts longer and may improve the taste of a food.	Hydrogenated fats have been linked to clogging the arteries and heart disease and should be avoided in the diet where possible. Many manufacturers have now removed all hydrogenated fats from their food.
Hydrogenated vegetable oil/fat	This is when *vegetable oil* has been chemically processed to make it harder, i.e. solid at room temperature. This means it lasts longer and may improve the taste of a food. May contain trans fatty acids (TFAs).	I found this in 25 out of 570 products I looked at. These were mostly cakes and biscuits. I found none used in the ready-meals or meat and fish products I looked at.
		Hydrogenated fats have been linked to clogging the arteries and heart disease and should

INGREDIENT	WHAT IS IT?	FURTHER INFORMATION
		be avoided in the diet where possible. Many manufacturers have now removed all hydrogenated fats from their food.
Hydrolysed rice protein	Hydrolysing is the process where a compound is split into its constituent parts by the action of water, often with the aid of an acid or alkali. The protein part of rice is split from the whole grain.	
Hydrolysed soya protein	See *hydrolysed vegetable protein*.	
Hydrolysed vegetable protein (HVP)	Hydrolysing is the process where a compound is split into its constituent parts by the action of water, often with the aid of an acid or alkali. The protein part of a vegetable source, usually *soya beans*, wheat, *rice* or *corn*, is split from the rest of the compound. This ingredient has many uses, including adding a base flavour to foods and as an *emulsifier*.	HVP is high in *glutamic acid*. Glutamic acid is a naturally occurring amino acid (protein) which is found in virtually all protein-containing foods, is manufactured by the body and is present in breast milk.
Hydroxy-propyl methyl cellulose E464	Made from *cellulose* this is used as a *stabiliser* and *emulsifier*.	This is an additive permitted in organic foods. For more information about organic foods see Chapter 2 and Appendix 2.

INGREDIENT	WHAT IS IT?	FURTHER INFORMATION
Icing sugar	This is powdered *granulated sugar*. An *anti-caking agent* is also usually included: *tricalcium phosphate* (E341) is the most common one.	
Indigo carmine E132	This is an artificial food colouring. It gives foods a blue colour. It is also known as *indigotine*.	I found it in 3 products, which were a cake mix and sweets. No supposed links to asthma, hyperactivity, allergic reactions and skin reactions have been scientifically proven. However, it is one of the food colours recommended by the Children's Hyperactivity Support Group be avoided in diets of sensitive children.
Indigotine E132	See *indigo carmine*.	
Inulin	This is a type of complex *sugar* and is found naturally in some plants. It is used to improve taste and to sweeten foods. The body is not able to fully digest it so it is a sugar with a reduced caloric value. It is also a natural *prebiotic*.	It is sometimes used in lower-calorie foods to give them a more acceptable and satisfying flavour.
Invert sugar	See *invert sugar syrup*.	
Invert sugar syrup	This is the mixture of *glucose* and *fructose* produced when	

	sucrose is hydrolysed, i.e. split into its individual components. It is sweeter than sucrose and is important in the manufacture of sweets as it prevents crystallisation.	
Iodine	This is a mineral which is important for the body for proper thyroid function. It is now added to salt as standard, and iodine deficiency is very rare. The thyroid glands help regulate the metabolism, i.e. our body's system for burning calories and converting them to energy.	
Iron	It is an essential mineral for the body involved in the transportation of oxygen around the body. It is found naturally in many foods such as red meat and leafy green vegetables and is commonly used to fortify foodstuffs such as breakfast cereals and breads.	See page 16 for Recommended Daily Amounts (RDA) for iron.
Iron oxides E172	These are naturally occurring red, brown, black, orange and yellow colours. They are used as natural food colourings.	
Iron sulphate	A form of iron which is commonly used to fortify foods and increase their iron content. See *iron* and *ferrous sulphate*.	

INGREDIENT	WHAT IS IT ?	FURTHER INFORMATION
Isolated soya protein/ soya protein isolate	Methods have been developed to remove just the protein part of the soya bean so it can be used on its own as a separate ingredient in foods. It is used to boost protein contents of foods but also to help hold foods together.	

INGREDIENT	WHAT IS IT?	FURTHER INFORMATION
Jalapeno	This is a medium- to large-sized green chilli pepper, commonly in Mexican foods.	
Jumbo oats	This is when the outer husk/shell of the oat grain has been removed but the oats have not been rolled, i.e. flattened into flakes. More of the nutritional value remains intact.	Oats are a rich source of *vitamin B1*, and a good source of protein, *iron*, *zinc* and *dietary fibre*.

INGREDIENT	WHAT IS IT?	FURTHER INFORMATION
Kidney bean	This is the ripe seed of a plant. It is found in dishes such as chilli con carne.	Kidney beans are a rich source of protein, *vitamin B1*, *folate*, *iron* and *selenium*, a good source of *vitamin B6* and *zinc* and a source of calcium. They are low in *fat* and rich in *dietary fibre*.

INGREDIENT	WHAT IS IT?	FURTHER INFORMATION
L. acidophilus (Lactobacillus acidophilus)	This is a *probiotic*, which are natural bacteria found in our bodies and important for a healthy-functioning digestive system. These bacteria are sometimes cultivated in a laboratory and then added to foods known as Functional Foods.	For more information about Functional Foods see Chapter 2.
Lactic acid E270	Lactic acid is produced by the fermentation of *carbohydrates* and was originally discovered in soured milk. It is what gives the flavour to fermented milk. It is able to suppress bacterial growth and is added to foods as a *preservative*. It is also added to give acidity and flavouring to foods.	I found lactic acid in many foods, including dairy products, sweets, soft drinks, sauces and condiments. This is an additive permitted in organic foods. For more information about organic foods see Chapter 2 and Appendix 2.
Lactic acid esters of mono-and di-glycerides of fatty acids E472b	Made from lactic acid this is used as an *emulsifier* and *stabiliser*.	
Lactic starter culture	This is derived from *lactic acid* and is added to a food to ferment it or make it sour. Used in products such as *crème fraîche*.	

INGREDIENT	WHAT IS IT?	FURTHER INFORMATION
Lactose	Lactose is the natural *sugar* found in milk and milk products such as *whey*. It is used in the pharmaceutical industry as a filler in tablets. It is less sweet than *sucrose* (about 16–20% of the sweetness). It is found naturally in all dairy products and milk but is also used as an ingredient and is added to foods as a sweetener.	Some people cannot digest lactose and are said to have what is known as a lactose intolerance.
L-cysteine E920	This is synthetically produced from the amino acid cysteine. It is used as a *flour treatment angent.*	
Lecithin E322	This is a natural substance usually derived from *soya beans*, egg yolk or sunflower oil. Used in food processing as an *emulsifier*.	This is a very common ingredient and is found in almost all chocolate products. This is an additive permitted in organic foods. For more information about organic foods see Chapter 2 and Appendix 2.
Lemon juice	This is sometimes added for flavour and sometimes to act as a natural *preservative* and stop food discolouring when exposed to the air.	
Lemon powder	This is when lemon juice is dehydrated, i.e. all the water is removed and it becomes a powder. This is added as a *flavouring*.	
Lime juice from concentrate	See *fruit juice from concentrate*.	

INGREDIENT	WHAT IS IT?	FURTHER INFORMATION
Linoleic acid	This is a *polyunsaturated* fatty acid which is also an *essential fatty acid* known also as *omega 6*. It is present in most vegetable oils.	
Locust bean gum E410	This is a gum extracted from the seeds of the carob tree. It is used as an *emulsifier* and *stabiliser* in foods. Also known as *carob bean gum*.	I found this in many children's yogurts. This is an additive permitted in organic foods. For more information on organic foods see Chapter 2 and Appendix 2.
Lovage	This is a herb and is used to add flavour to foods.	
Low-sodium sea salt	This is a natural sea salt rather than a chemically produced salt and has lower amounts of sodium and higher amounts of other minerals such as potassium and magnesium.	Sodium is the part of salt which it is advisable to reduce as part of a healthy balanced diet.
Lupin protein	This is a protein which is extracted from lupin seeds grown on lupin plants.	
Lutein E161b	This is one of the most widespread naturally occurring carotenoids (yellow-orange pigments) found in fruits and vegetables. This is used as a natural food colouring.	

INGREDIENT	WHAT IS IT?	FURTHER INFORMATION
Macaroni	This is a type of pasta and is often made from *durum wheat*.	
Mace	This is a spice which comes from the nutmeg tree (from which nutmeg also comes). It is used as a natural flavouring in foods.	
Mace extract	Mace extract is the concentrated form of mace i.e. from which the water has been removed. It is used as a natural flavouring in foods.	
Magnesium carbonate E504	This is synthetically made and is used as a buffer or neutraliser in foods. Common in baking powder and custard.	This additive is permitted in organic foods. For more information about organic foods see Chapter 2 and Appendix 2.
Maize	See *corn*.	
Maize flour	See *corn flour*.	
Maize starch	See *corn flour*.	
Malic acid E296	This is an acid which occurs naturally in many fruits and is used as an additive to increase the acidity of foods.	
Malt	Malt is derived from maltose (which is a sugar found in grains such as barley or wheat).	

INGREDIENT	WHAT IS IT?	FURTHER INFORMATION
Malted barley extract	*Malt* is derived from maltose (which is a sugar found in grains such as barley or wheat). It can be used to help sweeten foods and improve flavour.	I found it used as a flavouring in breakfast cereals.
Malt extract	*Malt* is derived from maltose (which is a sugar found in grains such as barley or wheat). It can be left as a liquid or dried into a powder. It is used as a *flavouring*.	
Maltitol E965	This is a sweetener derived from maltose (natural sugar found in the barley and wheat grains). It is 10% less sweet than *sucrose*. It digests slowly and is often used as a sweetener. Commonly used in children's medicines, chewing gum and sugar-free sweets.	I found it in all 7 children's medicines I looked at.
Maltodextrin	This is a complex *carbohydrate* found in malt. *Malt* is derived from the natural sugar maltose found in barley and wheat.	
Manioc starch	Manioc is another name for cassava. Manioc starch is a *carbohydrate* found in the manioc roots and is also called *tapioca starch*. This is used as a *bulking agent* and contains very few nutrients.	
Mannitol E421	This is a *sugar* found naturally in some vegetables but is usually commercially derived from seaweed. It is about 60% as sweet as sugar and used as	For more information about Sweeteners see Chapter 2 (Sweeteners).

INGREDIENT	WHAT IS IT?	FURTHER INFORMATION
	a sweetener in foods. Commonly used in chewing gum and sugar-free sweets.	
Maple syrup	Maple syrup is a *sugar* derived from the maple tree. Most maple-flavoured syrups used in food manufacturing are artificial and do not come from a natural source, as it is cheaper to use *corn syrup* with artificial maple flavourings.	Maple syrup is about 60% *sucrose* so is a high-sugar product.
Marjoram	This is a herb which is used to add flavour to foods.	
Mascarpone	This is an Italian *cream cheese*.	
Mature Cheddar cheese powder	This is when mature Cheddar *cheese* has had the water content removed to form a powder. This extends the shelf life.	
Meat broth	This is another word for meat stock where bits of meat, bone and skin of an animal have been boiled in water and then sieved, leaving a meat stock. Used in gravies and sauces.	
Mechanically recovered	This term is usually used in relation to chicken or pork. It means that the meat contained in the product has been sucked off the bones of the animal with a high-pressure machine. This means that a product does not contain very high-quality meat.	In the past there was fear that mechanically recovered beef meat could contain small amounts of the spinal cord and so could be a possible source of BSE, which is why only pork and chicken are now processed in this way.

INGREDIENT	WHAT IS IT?	FURTHER INFORMATION
Methyl-cellulose E461	Made from *cellulose* this is used as a *stabiliser* and *emulsifier*.	
Methyl p-hydroxy-benzoate E218	This is one of the group of *preservatives* called benzoates which are derived from benzoic acid.	I found this in 3 out of 7 children's medicines I looked at. The Food Standards Agency currently advise that benzoates could make symptoms of asthma and eczema worse in children with these conditions. For more information on the benzoates see Chapter 2 ('Preservatives').
Milk calcium complex	Calcium derived from milk.	
Milk chocolate	Type of chocolate made by incorporating milk powders along with *sugar*, chocolate liquor and *cocoa butter* or *vegetable fat*.	
Milk fat	Fat present in milk, mainly in the form of emulsified milk fat globules.	
Milk ferments	Another name for the natural bacteria and yeasts which are used to ferment milk. Usually found in *cheese* products. A common one is *lactic acid*.	
Milk minerals concentrate	All minerals that are found naturally in milk and are derived from milk.	
Milk powder	Milk which has had the water content removed and	

INGREDIENT	WHAT IS IT?	FURTHER INFORMATION
	so is just in powder form. It has a long shelf life.	
Milk protein	When listed it means that just the protein from milk has been used.	
Milk solids	This refers to milk proteins and *carbohydrates*, not *fats*. Usually listed when chocolate is used as an ingredient. Listed as a percentage.	
Milk sugar	Also known as *lactose*.	
Millet	This is the seeds of a grass plant. It is used as a gluten-free alternative to grains like wheat.	It is sometimes used in the whole seeds form on products such as breads. It is a good source of protein and many vitamins and minerals.
Mineral water	This is water which, having surfaced at a natural spring, is then allowed to travel over rock before being collected. It therefore has a higher mineral content than *spring water*. It is not allowed to be treated in any way.	
Mixed carotenes E160a	Carotenes are a natural orange-red pigment found in some fruit and vegetables. Carotenes are used as a natural food colouring.	Found in many products from *cheese*, sweets and yogurts to savoury frozen foods.
Modified cornflour	'Modified' means that a substance has been changed by chemical or physical means to be better adapted for a particular function. See *corn*	

INGREDIENT	WHAT IS IT?	FURTHER INFORMATION
	flour. Used as a *bulking agent* or *thickener* in foods.	
Modified maize starch	Another name for *modified cornflour*.	
Modified potato starch	'Modified' means that a substance has been changed by chemical or physical means to be better adapted for a particular function. Used as a *bulking agent* or *thickener* in foods.	
Modified starch	'Modified' means that a substance has been changed by chemical or physical means to be better adapted for a particular function. Used as a *bulking agent* or *thickener* in foods. The term refers to any *starch* which has been changed to make it easier to use in food processing. Common starches used are corn, wheat and rice. Note that a product containing modified starch may contain *gluten*.	
Modified tapioca starch	'Modified' means that a substance has been changed by chemical or physical means to be better adapted for a particular function. See *manioc starch*. Used as a *bulking agent* or *thickener* in foods. Tapioca is a high-*carbohydrate* food which comes from the root of the manioc/cassava plant.	
Modified waxy maize starch	'Modified' means that a substance has been changed by chemical or physical means	

INGREDIENT	WHAT IS IT?	FURTHER INFORMATION
	to be better adapted for a particular function. See *corn flour*. Used as a *bulking agent* or *thickener* in foods.	
Modified wheat starch	'Modified' means that a substance has been changed by chemical or physical means to be better adapted for a particular function. Used as a *bulking agent* or *thickener* in foods.	
Molasses	Molasses is a thick syrup by-product of the processing of sugar cane and sugar beet into *sugar*. It contains nearly 70% *sucrose* plus some *glucose* and *fructose*.	It is a source of *iron* but only has traces of other minerals.
Mono-and diacetyl tartaric esters of mono- and diglycerides of fatty acids E472e	Made from *tartaric acid*, this is an *emulsifier* and *stabiliser*.	
Mono- and diglycerides of fatty acids E471	This additive is made from *glycerin* and fats. It is an *emulsifier*.	
Monocalcium phosphate E341a	Used as a *raising agent* in baking powder and self-raising flour.	This additive is permitted in organic foods. For more information about organic foods see Chapter 2 and Appendix 2.
Monosodium glutamate (MSG) E621	This is the sodium salt of *glutamic acid*. It is prepared synthetically for use in food production. It is used as a	I found MSG in 8 foods out of the 570 I looked at. These were a range of popular crisps, dried packet noodles,

INGREDIENT	WHAT IS IT?	FURTHER INFORMATION
	flavour enhancer in a range of foods and is also used in restaurants.	cured meats and one ready-meal.
Monterey Jack cheese	This is a semi-hard *cheese* similar to *mozzarella* but coming from California.	
Mozzarella cheese	This is a *cheese*.	
Muscovado sugar	This is a brown and sticky *sugar* which is the least refined (processed) of the table sugars.	
Mushroom juice	Liquid produced from mushrooms.	
Mustard flour	Mustard flour comes from the ground seeds of the mustard plant. It is used to add a natural flavour to foods.	
Mycoprotein	This is a commercially produced, vegetarian, high-protein substance made by fermenting fungi (mushrooms). It is used as a vegetarian source of protein in vegetarian meat-replacement dishes, e.g. burgers and sausages.	

INGREDIENT	WHAT IS IT?	FURTHER INFORMATION
Natural colouring	This is listed on an ingredients list when one of a number of food colours from natural sources have been used. The specific colouring is given on the label as well.	
Natural flavourings	These are substances used to give flavour and/or smell to a product. Under EU legislation the expression 'Natural Flavourings' can only be used on those extracted from vegetable or animal materials. The specific flavouring used in a product does not have to be listed under current EU legislation. There are over 2,500 flavourings currently permitted in food use.	
Natural strawberry flavouring	This means that the flavouring used is either extracted from strawberries or is nature identical, i.e. made in a laboratory but chemically very similar.	
Natural vanilla flavouring	This means that the flavouring used is either extracted from vanilla pods or is nature identical, i.e. made in a laboratory but chemically very similar.	

INGREDIENT	WHAT IS IT?	FURTHER INFORMATION
Nettle	This is the young leaves of the stinging nettle plant. They are edible.	
Niacin	This is the technical name for *vitamin B3*. An essential vitamin involved in helping the body get energy from food. It is found naturally in many foods such as red meats, poultry, fish and nuts. It is used to fortify many foodstuffs, including breakfast cereals and breads.	
Nicotinamide	This is a technical name for *vitamin B3*.	
Noodles	These are ribbons of pasta made with *wheat* flour, water and sometimes *eggs*, and are common in Asian cooking. They can be of varying thickness. They can also be made using *rice* flour and *buckwheat* flour.	They are a complex carbohydrate food. For more information about complex carbohydrates see Chapter 3.
Nutmeg	Also known as *mace*.	

INGREDIENT	WHAT IS IT?	FURTHER INFORMATION
Oats	This is a *grain* cereal.	They are a rich source of *vitamin B1*, a good source of protein, *iron* and *zinc*, and a source of *niacin*. They also contain *dietary fibre*.
Oat flakes	Oat kernels which have been flattened and rolled into flake form.	
Oat flour	Ground oats with the outer bran layer removed from the grain.	
Oat meal	Another term for *rolled oats*.	
Oleic acids	This is a monounsaturated *fat* found in most fats; the richest sources are *olive oil* and *rapeseed oil*.	For more information about fats see Chapter 3.
Oligofructose	This is a natural plant *sugar* and has a sweet taste. It cannot be fully digested by the body and has a reduced calorific value. It is used as a sweetener in foods as well as a way of adding fibre — it is a rich source of fibre. It is also a *prebiotic*.	
Olive oil	This is an oil made from olives. Virgin olive oil means that the oil was extracted from olives using only physical means,	One of the richest sources of mono-unsaturated *fat* and so is beneficial to health.

INGREDIENT	WHAT IS IT?	FURTHER INFORMATION
	i.e. crushing. Refined olive oil means the oil has been treated chemically to neutralise the strong taste.	For more information about fats see Chapter 3.
Omega 3 from fish oil	See *omega-3 oils*.	
Omega-3 oils	These oils are found in oily fish (such as salmon, tuna, herring, trout, sardines and mackerel). They are what is known as *essential fatty acids*, which means that the body cannot produce them so we have to get them from the food we eat.	Research indicates that they may have health benefits, in particular for heart health. There has been recent research looking at the role that these oils may play in brain development in children and also whether they can help with behavioural difficulties. For more information about omega 3 oils see Chapters 2 and 3.
Omega-6 oils	These oils are found in vegetable sources such as seeds (sunflowers), *wheat germ*, *avocado* and nuts. They are an *essential fatty acid*, which means the body cannot produce them, so we need to get them from the food we eat.	Research indicates that they may have health benefits, in particular for heart health.
Onion powder	Dried onions are ground into a fine powder. It is usually used to add flavour.	
Orange comminute from concentrate	Comminute is when the whole fruit is pulverised. Some of the water is then removed from the juice part to create a concentrated substance. This can help the juice be transported long distances,	

	sometimes across the world. Once in the UK the water is added back to the concentrate again along with the solids e.g. pith.	
Orange juice from concentrate	See *fruit juice from concentrate*.	
Orange oil	This is when the natural oils from the orange fruit have been extracted. The oil is very concentrated in flavour and is used as a natural flavouring.	
Oregano	This is a herb commonly added to the top of pizzas and Italian foods. It is used to add flavour to foods.	
Organic	See Chapter 2 (What Does Organic Mean?) and Appendix 2 for more information.	

INGREDIENT	WHAT IS IT?	FURTHER INFORMATION
Palm oil	A vegetable oil derived from the palm tree. It is the most widely used oil in the world in food manufacturing. High in *beta-carotenes* (vegetable form of *vitamin A*) and so has an orange colour, but these are usually removed to produce a pale oil.	Palm oil is 45% saturated, 40% monounsaturated and about 10% polyunsaturated. It is therefore richer in saturated fats than most other vegetable oils.
Pantothenic acid	Otherwise known as vitamin B5 it is an essential vitamin and helps the body get energy from food. Found naturally in many foods such as wholegrains, eggs, beans and pulses.	
Paprika extract E160c	Paprika is a natural food colouring made from the pigment of red *bell pepper*. It is also used as a natural flavouring. It is also called capsanthin.	I found it used in savoury products, crisps, ready-meals and sweets.
Parsley	This is a herb which is used to add natural flavour to foods.	
Partially hydrogenated vegetable oil	This is when vegetable oil has been chemically processed to make it harder at room temperature. This helps it to have a longer shelf life and be more stable. It may contain trans fatty acids (TFAs).	Hydrogenated *fats* have been linked to clogging the arteries and heart disease and should be avoided in the diet where possible. Many manufacturers have now removed all hydrogenated fats from their food.

INGREDIENT	WHAT IS IT?	FURTHER INFORMATION
Partially inverted brown sugar syrup	This is the mixture of *glucose* and *fructose* produced when *sucrose* is *hydrolysed*, i.e. split into its individual components. It is sweeter than sucrose and is important in the manufacture of sweets as it prevents crystallisation. When made using brown sugar it means that the syrup is less refined i.e. less processed than white sugar.	
Partially inverted refiners syrup	This is the mixture of *glucose* and *fructose* produced when *sucrose* is *hydrolysed*, i.e. split into its individual components. It is sweeter than sucrose and is important in the manufacture of sweets as it prevents crystallisation.	
Partially reconstituted milk protein	*Milk protein* is listed when the manufacturer has just used the protein content of milk. The water content is then removed to form a milk-protein powder. 'Partially reconstituted' means that some (but not all) of the water has been added to the milk-protein powder again. This is used as a milk alternative and to add protein.	
Partially reconstituted whey powder	This is when some (but not all) of the water is added back to dried *whey* or *whey powder*.	
Partially reconstituted whey protein	This is when some (but not all) of the water is added back to dried *whey* protein.	

INGREDIENT	WHAT IS IT?	FURTHER INFORMATION
Partially rehydrated dried potato	This is when some (but not all) of the water is added back to dehydrated potato.	
Passata	This is a tomato sauce commonly used to top pizzas. It is usually just tomatoes which have been puréed until smooth.	
Pasteurised	Pasteurising is the process of making milk and other liquids such as fruit juices safe for consumption by destroying most of the micro-organisms in them. It is a means of lengthening the storage time of a product. This is done through heating.	Some of the nutritional value of foods may be lost during the heating process, e.g. some *vitamin C* is lost when heated so fruit juices which have been pasteurised may have lower vitamin C levels.
Pasteurised egg white	See *pasteurised*.	
Pasteurised egg yolk	See *pasteurised*.	
Pasteurised whole egg	See *pasteurised*.	
Patent blue V E131	This is an artificial food colouring. It gives foods a dark-violet colour.	I found it in 3 products, which were a cake mix and sweets.

No supposed links to asthma, hyperactivity, allergic reactions and skin reactions have been scientifically proven. However, it is one of the food colours recommended by the Children's Hyperactivity Support Group be avoided in diets of sensitive children. |

INGREDIENT	WHAT IS IT?	FURTHER INFORMATION
Peach purée	See *fruit purée*.	
Pea fibre	This is when the part of the pea which is rich in fibre (usually the outer skin) has been added to a food.	
Peanuts	Peanuts are also known as groundnuts and monkey nuts. They are ground to oil which is commonly used in food processing and restaurants (particularly in Asian food). Peanuts are the most common nut allergen and current advice is for pregnant and lactating women and children up to the age of 3 to avoid them if there is a history of allergies in the family. In their whole-nut form peanuts can be a choking hazard for young children.	Peanuts are a rich source of protein, *niacin* and *vitamin E* and *vitamin B1*. They are also a good source of zinc. Dry-roasted or roasted and salted peanuts are much lower in vitamin B1 and contain a high amount of salt. Peanuts are about 30% *fat* of which 20% is saturated and 50% mono-unsaturated.
Pear extracts	See *fruit extracts*.	
Pea starch	This is a complex *sugar* which is derived from peas. It is used as a *bulking agent*.	
Pecan nuts	These grow on an American tree. They are found in breakfast cereals, muesli, cereal bars and cakes.	Pecan nuts are a rich source of selenium, *vitamin E* and *niacin*, a good source of *vitamin B1* and *zinc* and a source of protein. They are about 40% *fat* of which 10% is saturated and 60% is mono-unsaturated.
Pectin E440	This is a complex *carbohydrate* found in all plant cell walls.	This is an additive permitted in organic foods. For more

INGREDIENT	WHAT IS IT?	FURTHER INFORMATION
	Major sources are apples and citrus fruits. Pectins are used in the food industry as *gelling agents*, *stabilisers* and *thickeners*. Found commonly in jams and jellies.	information on organic foods see Chapter 2 and Appendix 2.
Penta sodium triphosphate E451	This is an *emulsifier* in foods and is found in products such as *cheese*.	
Peppercorns	These are berries which are dried and ground to produce black pepper or white pepper (the outer dark-coloured skins are removed first). Used to add flavour to food.	
Pepper extract	This is when the oil is extracted from peppercorns. It is intense in flavour.	
Phenylalanine	Phenylalanine is one of the amino acids used to make *aspartame*. It is an essential amino acid (we must get it from the diet as the body cannot make it).	A very small number of people with the genetic disorder phenylketonuria (PKU) cannot metabolise phenylalanine from any source whatsoever and must restrict their intake. This is why products containing aspartame have the sentence 'Contains a source of phenylalanine' on the label by law. It is not possible to have PKU and not be aware of the fact.
Phosphoric acid E338	This is used as an *acidity regulator*. Common in fizzy drinks.	I found this in just one cola product. There have been links to dental erosion and loss of calcium from the body but this has not been scientifically proven.

INGREDIENT	WHAT IS IT?	FURTHER INFORMATION
Pimiento	This is the Spanish name for pepper.	
Pineapple juice	This is juice extracted from pineapples.	
Pineapple juice from concentrate	See *fruit juice from concentrate*	
Plain (spirit) caramel E150a	This is one of four caramel colourants used by food manufacturers, ranging from light brown to very dark brown in colour. They are produced by heating *carbohydrates* (e.g. *sugars* or malt syrups) in the presence of small amounts of food-grade acids, alkalis or salts. These colours are the most commonly used colourants in food. Caramel is also used in *flavourings*.	Research into this food colourant and a link to asthma and skin irritation has not been scientifically conclusive. However, this is one of the food colours the Children's Hyperactivity Support Group recommends is avoided by sensitive children. I found this food colour in just over 60% of the products I looked at which contained food colours.
Plain chocolate	A confectionery product made from fermented and roasted cocoa beans blended with *sugar*, *cocoa butter* and *lecithins*. Contains no milk.	
Polyglycerol esters of fatty acids E475	This is a synthetic *emulsifier* and *stabiliser*.	
Polyglycerol polyricinoleate E476	Made from castor oil this is a *stabiliser* and *emulsifier*.	

Polyoxy-ethylene sorbitanmono-stearate **E436**	This is derived from *sorbitol* and is an *emulsifier* and *stabiliser*. Also known as *polysorbate 60*.	
Polyphos-phates **E452**	This is often listed as an *emulsifying salt*, i.e. it can help a food to be heated and not go stringy or helps ingredients to bind. Commonly used in processed cheeses to help ingredients bind together.	
Polysorbate 60 **E436**	This is derived from *sorbitol* and is an *emulsifier* and *stabiliser*. Also known as *polyoxyethylene sorbitan monostearate*.	
Ponceau 4R **E124**	This is an artificial *azo dye* food colouring permitted in food use. It gives a strawberry-red colour.	This is one of five food colourants which the Food Standards Agency in the UK is currently recommending should be avoided if your child shows symptoms of hyperactivity. For more information see Chapter 2 (Colourings). This is one of the food additives currently under review by the European Food Safety Authority. This may lead to a change in regulation sometime in 2008. For updated information about this food dye see the website www.whatsinthis.co.uk. I found it in 1 out of the 570 products I looked at and this was a confectionery item.

INGREDIENT	WHAT IS IT?	FURTHER INFORMATION
Popping corn	Natural *corn* kernels which are used to make popcorn.	
Pork	Meat from pigs.	
Pork belly	This is the meat around the stomach area of the cow. It is what lardons are made from.	
Pork fat	When extra fat derived from pork is used.	
Pork gelatin	This is a soluble protein prepared from collagen (a component found in animal skin, e.g. pig) or bones by boiling with water. It is used as *gelling agent* in sugar confectionery, jellies, ice cream, yogurt, fresh fruit cakes and in tinned meats. It is also used in the pharmaceutical industry in capsules.	
Pork rind	This is the cooked skin of pig meat. It is sometimes added to sausages.	
Potassium carbonate E501	This is a salt of potassium. It is used as a buffer and neutralising agent.	This additive is permitted in organic foods. For more information about organic foods see Chapter 2 and Appendix 2.
Potassium chloride E508	This is a natural salt used in salt-substitute products.	
Potassium citrate E332	This is a salt of citric acid and is used as an *acidity regulator* and *emulsifier*.	

INGREDIENT	WHAT IS IT?	FURTHER INFORMATION
Potassium diphosphate E450 (a)	Made synthetically and used for its ability as a *gelling agent*, *emulsifier* and *stabiliser*.	I found this in cheese products.
Potassium iodide	This is the potassium salt of *iodine*.	
Potassium lactate E326	This is the potassium salt of *lactic acid* and acts as a buffer in foods.	
Potassium nitrate E252	This occurs naturally in plants and is used as a *preservative* in cured meats.	I found it in 5 out of 570 products and these were all cured meats such as bacon and pepperoni and pasta ready-meals and pizzas containing these. This additive is permitted in organic foods. For more information about organic foods see Chapter 2 and Appendix 2.
Potassium nitrite E249	A natural *preservative* used in cured and smoked foods.	I found it in 2 out of 570 products and these were both products containing cured meats.
Potassium sorbate E202	This is a synthetically made *preservative* which is used for its antibacterial and antifungal properties.	I found this was the most common preservative used in the 570 products I looked at. I found it in meat products, drinks and cakes.
Potassium tartrate E336	Known more simply as *cream of tartar* it is commonly added to foods as a *raising agent*.	This additive is permitted in organic foods. For more information about organic foods see Chapter 2 and Appendix 2.
Potatoes	Potatoes are a root vegetable. They are used in many ready-	They are a *carbohydrate* food and are a good source of

INGREDIENT	WHAT IS IT?	FURTHER INFORMATION
	meals as well as in granule and powder forms in foods.	*vitamin C* and *vitamin B6*. They also contain *dietary fibre*, particularly in the skins.
Potato granules	These are produced from dehydrated/dried potatoes. Used in savoury snacks.	
Potato powder	This is produced from dehydrated/dried potatoes. Used in savoury snacks.	
Potato starch	Starch from potatoes used as a *stabiliser*.	
Prebiotics	These are nondigestible complex *sugars* found naturally in some foods. They promote the growth of healthy bacteria in our bodies. Examples of prebiotics are *inulin* and *fructo-oligosaccharides*.	They are seen as potentially beneficial for health and are added to Functional Foods. For more information about Functional Foods see Chapter 2.
Preservatives	These are a large group of additives that help to keep food safe to consume for longer. They have a number of roles from stopping the growth of harmful bacteria and fungi to stopping foods from going rancid. They include the groups of preservatives known as sulphites and benzoates. Natural preservatives include *salt*, *sugar* and *vinegar*.	
Probiotic live cultures	These are bacteria which benefit health by promoting	They are sometimes added to foods, e.g. Functional Foods.

INGREDIENT	WHAT IS IT?	FURTHER INFORMATION
	a balanced gastrointestinal tract.	For more information about Functional Foods see Chapter 2.
Processed cheese	This is a product made from one or more cheeses and emulsifiers, ingredients such as *whey* or *milk*, *flavourings* and sometimes added food colourings.	Check the cheese contents as these differ widely. Not as rich in nutrients as natural cheese.
Propane-1,2-diol esters of fatty acids E477	An *emulsifier*, i.e. helps ingredients to mix well that usually wouldn't, such as oil and water.	
Propyl gallate E310	This comes from gallic acid, which is an acid produced artificially and it is added to foods as an *antioxidant*, especially in fats (as it is soluble in fats).	
Propyl p-hydroxy-benzoate E216	This is one of the group of *preservatives* called benzoates, which are derived from benzoic acid.	I found this in 3 out of 7 children's medicines I looked at. The Food Standards Agency currently advise that benzoates could make symptoms of asthma and eczema worse in children with these conditions. For more information on the benzoates see Chapter 2 ('Preservatives').
Provolone cheese	This is an Italian *cheese* which is similar to *mozzarella*.	
Puffed oats	All puffed grains are made by heating the grain in a sealed container until it explodes.	

INGREDIENT	WHAT IS IT?	FURTHER INFORMATION
Pumpkin seeds	Seeds produced by pumpkins, the starchy vegetable.	They are rich in unsaturated *fats*. For more information about fats see Chapter 3.
Pyrodoxine hydrochloride	This is the technical name for *Vitamin B6*. An essential vitamin involved in helping the body get energy from food. It is found naturally in many foods such as wholegrains, meats, fish, *wheat germ* and yeasts. It is used to fortify many foodstuffs, including breakfast cereals and breads.	

INGREDIENT	WHAT IS IT?	FURTHER INFORMATION
Quinoa	Pronounced keen-wah, this is a grain like wheat, only it is *gluten* free and higher in protein than many grains. It comes originally from South America.	Quinoa is a rich source of *iron* and *vitamin B1* and a source of *protein*, *calcium*, *niacin* and *vitamin B2*. I found it in some infant weaning foods.
Quinoline yellow E104	This is an artificial *azo dye* food colouring permitted for use in foods. It is a yellow colour.	This is one of five food colourants which the Food Standards Agency in the UK is currently recommending should be avoided if your child shows symptoms of hyperactivity. For more information see Chapter 2 (Colourings). This is one of the food additives currently under review by the European Food Safety Authority. This may lead to a change in regulation sometime in 2008. For updated information about this food dye see the website www.whatsinthis.co.uk. I found it in 7 out of the 570 products I looked at, and these were cake mixes, sweets and confectionery.

INGREDIENT	WHAT IS IT?	FURTHER INFORMATION
Raising agents	These include familiar substances like baking powder (sodium bicarbonate), which helps foods such as bread and cakes to rise. They are used for home baking as well as in the manufacturing industry.	
Raisins	Raisins are dried grapes. See *dried fruit* also.	Raisins are a source of *dietary fibre*. They are a concentrated source of fruit sugars.
Rapeseed oil	Rapeseed is a plant from the mustard and cabbage family. It is a very commonly used vegetable oil in food production.	Rapeseed oil is 60% monounsaturated fat, 33% polyunsaturated fat and only 7% saturated *fat*. For more information on fats see Chapter 3.
Raspberry purée	See *fruit purée*.	
Ravioli	This is a type of pasta made from *durum wheat* or *durum wheat semolina*.	
Raw sugar	This is brown unrefined *sugar*, usually imported in this state and then refined into white sugar in the UK.	
Reconstituted dried skimmed milk	This is dried skimmed-milk powder which has had some of the water added back into it.	

INGREDIENT	WHAT IS IT?	FURTHER INFORMATION
Reconstituted egg white	This is dried egg white which has had the water added back to it.	
Reconstituted tomato purée	This is when the water content has been removed from pulped tomatoes to create a concentrated tomato purée and then the water has been added back to it again.	
Reconstituted whole egg	This is dried whole egg which has had the water added back to it.	
Reconstituted whole milk	This is whole-milk powder which has had water added back to it.	
Red rice koji	This is a type of rice with a red colour which has been fermented with alcohol or sugar.	
Reduced-fat cheese	This is natural *cheese* which has had some of the fat content removed from it.	
Reduced sodium mineral salt	This means that the *salt* used in the product has a greater amount of *potassium chloride* than sodium chloride.	
Red wine	This is sometimes used to help flavour foods. When wine is cooked the alcohol part of it evaporates so no alcohol is present in the food.	
Refined	Refining is the removal of impurities or unwanted elements from a substance.	

INGREDIENT	WHAT IS IT?	FURTHER INFORMATION
	Often used to describe the processing of oils and sugars.	
Refined fish oil	Refining is the process of removing impurities. Fish oil is a source of *omega-3 oils*, which are a type of *polyunsaturated fat*. They have been proven to be beneficial for the body.	
Rehydrated soya protein	This is when dried *soya protein* has the water added back to it. This ingredient is sometimes used in vegetarian meat-replacement foods, as it provides a good vegetarian protein source.	
Rehydrated wheat protein	This is when dried wheat protein has the water added back to it. This ingredient is sometimes used as a protein in vegetarian meat-replacement foods.	
Riboflavin E101	This is a natural yellow-orange food colouring. It is also the technical term for *vitamin B2*.	I found this colouring used in a number of products such as yogurts and sweets.
Rice	Rice is a grain. It is covered with a fibrous husk which is about 40% of the grain. When this is removed, *brown rice* is left. When the outer bran layers are removed, polished white rice is left. It is *gluten* free.	Polished white rice is a source of *niacin* and *protein*.
Rice flour	Raw rice grains can be ground into a flour and used as a natural thickener. It is *gluten*	

	free. Rice flour can also be used to make cakes, biscuits and breads as an alternative to wheat flours. Commonly found in gluten-free products, e.g. bread, cakes, breakfast cereals and pastas. It is also used to make rice noodles.	
Rice protein	This appears when just the protein part of the rice grain has been used in the food.	
Rice starch	The starch part of the rice grain is used on its own in foods, sometimes as a natural *thickener*. It is *gluten* free.	
Risotto rice	This is a type of rice which is higher in *carbohydrate* than normal rice, so it sticks together more and thickens when cooked. Used to make risotto dishes and paella.	
Rolled oats	Whole oat flakes are flattened or rolled into smaller thinner flakes.	
Rosemary extract	A natural oil from the rosemary herb.	
Rusk from wheat	This is a cereal which is added to foods as a *bulking agent*. Usually found in meat products such as sausages and hamburgers.	
Rye	This is a grain which is *gluten* free.	

INGREDIENT	WHAT IS IT?	FURTHER INFORMATION
Rye flour	This is ground rye grain. It is sometimes used in multigrain products or in wheat and *gluten*-free products as a replacement to wheat.	

S

INGREDIENT	WHAT IS IT?	FURTHER INFORMATION
Saccharin E954	Saccharin is an artificial sweetener which is 300–550 times sweeter than *sucrose*. It is non-calorific as it does not get digested by the body but just passes straight through.	I found sodium saccharin (which is the sodium salt of saccharin) in 8 out of 570 products. Two of these were children's medicines and the rest were sugar-free drinks and cordials.
Saccharose	This is the official chemical name for table *sugar*, so it basically means table sugar.	
Safflower	This is a plant which is used for its oil as well as being a natural yellow food colouring.	
Sage extract	Sage is a herb used as a natural flavouring.	
Salt	Salt has many uses: to preserve food; to improve taste; to help texturise and bind food; to control fermentation in foods such as breads. Salt is also called *sodium chloride*, which is a natural mineral and it's the sodium in salt that is not good for health if eaten in excess. The body requires the mineral sodium for many functions.	For more information about salt and daily maximum amounts see Chapter 3.
Sea salt	This is a natural salt derived from the sea as opposed to table salt, which is typically mined from the ground.	

INGREDIENT	WHAT IS IT?	FURTHER INFORMATION
Seasoning	Seasoning is the process of adding or improving flavours of food. The most common ones are salt and pepper.	
Semolina	Semolina is a part of the wheat grain which is sometimes used in breads and pasta. It has a coarse texture and a yellow colour.	
Sesame oil	This is the naturally extracted oil from sesame seeds. It is used commonly in stir-fries and Chinese and Thai cooking.	It is rich in polyunsaturated *fat* and low in saturated fat.
Shellac E904	This is a natural resin derived from an insect. It is used for coatings of foods such as fruits, chocolate and confectionery.	
Silicon dioxide E551	Also known as silica, which is a mineral, this is a natural *anti-caking* and *thickening agent*.	This additive is permitted in organic foods. For more information about organic foods see Chapter 2 and Appendix 2.
Single cream	This is cream with a minimum fat content of 18%.	
Skimmed milk powder	Skimmed milk which has been dried to a powder form. Contains all the nutritional content of skimmed milk. Fluid milk contains approximately 88% water. The benefits of this ingredient include increased shelf life, convenience, product flexibility, decreased transportation costs and storage.	

INGREDIENT	WHAT IS IT?	FURTHER INFORMATION
Smoked foods	Smoking is a process of flavouring, preserving or cooking foods by exposing it to smoke from burning plant matter, commonly wood.	Smoked foods commonly also contain *sodium* and *potassium nitrates* and nitrites as preservatives (E249 – E252).
Smoke flavouring	*Flavourings* produced by contact of a liquid, usually water or oils, with smoke produced by the burning of wood.	
Sodium	Sodium is a dietary essential mineral. *Sodium chloride* is most commonly found in the form of *salt*.	For more information about salt, sodium and daily maximum amounts see Chapter 3.
Sodium 5'-ribonucleotide E635	This is a synthetically made *flavour enhancer*.	I found this in 3 types of crisps.
Sodium acetate E262	This is the sodium salt of *acetic acid*. Used as an *acidity regulator*. Also known as *sodium diacetate*.	
Sodium alginate E401	The sodium salt of alginic acid. Used as a *stabiliser*.	This is an additive permitted in organic foods. For more information about organic foods see Chapter 2 and Appendix 2.
Sodium aluminium phosphate E541	This is a synthetically made substance used as a *raising agent* in foods and to increase the acidity of a food.	
Sodium ascorbate E301	This is the sodium salt of *ascorbic acid*. It is used as an *antioxidant* and *preservative*.	This additive is permitted in organic foods. For more information about organic foods see Chapter 2 and Appendix 2.

INGREDIENT	WHAT IS IT?	FURTHER INFORMATION
Sodium benzoate E211	This is one of the group of *preservatives* called benzoates which are derived from benzoic acid.	I found this in 6 out of 570 products I looked at. All but one of these were soft drinks and cordials.
		The Food Standards Agency currently advise that benzoates could make symptoms of asthma and eczema worse in children with these conditions.
		This additive is also recommended by the Children's Hyperactivity Support Group to be avoided by sensitive children.
		For more information on the benzoates see Chapter 2 ('Preservatives').
Sodium bicarbonate E500	Used as a *raising agent* in breads and many baked foods. Also known as *sodium carbonate*. More commonly known as baking powder.	This is an additive permitted in organic foods. For more information about organic foods see Chapter 2 and Appendix 2.
Sodium bisulphite E222	This is one of a group of *sulphites* that are used as food *preservatives*. If a product contains sulphites at levels above 10mg per kg this legally has to be labelled on the product.	Sulphites have been scientifically proven to be able to trigger asthma so they are best avoided if your child suffers from asthma.
		This additive is also one recommended by the Children's Hyperactivity Support Group to be avoided by sensitive children.
Sodium carbonate E500	Also known as *sodium bicarbonate* or more commonly known as baking powder.	This is an additive permitted in organic foods. For more information about organic foods see Chapter 2 and Appendix 2.

INGREDIENT	WHAT IS IT?	FURTHER INFORMATION
Sodium chloride	*Salt* is the commonest form in which sodium is consumed. Sodium chloride is the chemical name for salt.	
Sodium citrate E331	This is the salt of *citric acid*. It is a natural *acidity regulator*.	This is an additive permitted in organic foods. For more information about organic foods see Chapter 2 and Appendix 2.
Sodium diacetate E262	This is the sodium salt of *acetic acid*. Used as an *acidity regulator*. Also known as *sodium acetate*.	
Sodium diphosphates E450	These are a group of additives used mainly in *cheese* products. They change the texture and properties of the cheese so that it can be heated without going stringy, as well as help the mixing process when two different types of cheese are mixed together. Also known as an *emulsifying salt*.	
Sodium erythorbate E316	This is added to foods as an *antioxidant*.	
Sodium hydrogen carbonate E500	Also called *sodium bicarbonate* and *sodium carbonate*, which are both other names used for baking powder.	
Sodium lactate E325	This is a natural salt derived from *lactic acid*. It is sometimes used in confectionery to 'buffer' lactic acid, which then means that a very clear sweet can be produced.	This is an additive permitted in organic foods. For more information about organic foods see Chapter 2 and Appendix 2.

INGREDIENT	WHAT IS IT?	FURTHER INFORMATION
Sodium meta-bisulphite E223	This is one of a group of *sulphites* that are used as food *preservatives*. If a product contains sulphites at levels above 10mg per kg this legally has to be labelled on the product	This was the most commonly used sulphite I found and it was in 17 out of 570 products. These were cordials and sugar-free drinks, meat products, fresh filled pasta and varieties of crisps. Sulphites have been scientifically proven to be able to trigger asthma so they are best avoided if your child suffers from asthma. This additive is also one recommended by the Children's Hyperactivity Support Group to be avoided by sensitive children.
Sodium nitrate E252	This occurs naturally in plants and is used as a preservative in cured meats.	I found this in 2 products, which were both cured meats. This additive is permitted in organic foods. For more information about organic foods see Chapter 2 and Appendix 2.
Sodium nitrite E250	A natural preservative used in cured and smoked foods.	I found this in 9 products, which were either cured meats, smoked foods or foods containing these. This additive is permitted in organic foods. For more information about organic foods see Chapter 2 and Appendix 2.
Sodium ortho-phosphates E450	Additives used mainly in *cheese* products. They change the texture and properties of the cheese so that it can be heated without going stringy, as well as help the mixing process when two different types of	

INGREDIENT	WHAT IS IT?	FURTHER INFORMATION
	cheese are mixed together. Also known as an *emulsifying salt*, it is derived from phosphate.	
Sodium phosphate/ sodium polyphos- phates E339	Additives used mainly in *cheese* products. They change the texture and properties of the cheese so that it can be heated without going stringy, as well as help the mixing process when two different types of cheese are mixed together. Also known as an *emulsifying salt* and derived from phosphate.	
Sodium saccharin E954	*Saccharin* is 550 times sweeter than table *sugar* and so it is used as a sweetener in foods. However, as it does not get digested by the body but just passes straight through, it provides the body with no energy, i.e. no calories. Sodium saccharin is the most commonly used form of saccharin in food and drinks, as it is water-soluble. It is also used in sugar-free medicines.	I found sodium saccharin (which is the sodium salt of saccharin) in 8 out of 570 products. Two of these were children's medicines and the rest were sugar-free drinks and cordials.
Sodium stearoyl 2-lactylate E481	Made from *lactic acid*, this is a *stabiliser* and *emulsifier*.	
Sodium triphosphates E450	Additives used commonly in *cheese* and processed meat products. They change the texture and properties of the cheese so that it can be heated without going stringy, as well as help the mixing process when	

INGREDIENT	WHAT IS IT?	FURTHER INFORMATION
	two different types of cheese are mixed together. Also known as an *emulsifying salt* and derived from phosphate.	
Sorbic acid E200	This is an acid which can be extracted from berries or made chemically. It inhibits growth of moulds and bacteria in foods, so is used as a *preservative*.	
Sorbitan mono-stearate E491	Made from stearic acid, it is found in most animal and vegetable fats. It is used as a *glazing agent*, *emulsifier* and *stabiliser*.	
Sorbitan tristearate E492	Made from stearic acid, it is found in most vegetable fats. It is used as an *emulsifier* and *stabiliser*.	
Sorbitol E420	Used as a sweetener. It is a bulk sweetener and is 50–60% less sweet than *sucrose*. It is also digested slowly, unlike sucrose. It is used in sugar-free drinks, sweets and children's medicines.	I found it in 2 children's medicines out of the 570 products I looked at. In large amounts this can have a laxative effect. For more information about sweeteners see Chapter 2 (Sweeteners).
Soya beans	These are the beans which come from the soya plant. They are a source of vegetarian protein and a vegetable oil. Soya is very widely used and about two-thirds of all processed foods contain soya in some form.	Soya beans are a good source of *protein* and *iron*, a source of *niacin* and *calcium* and also provide some *dietary fibre*.

INGREDIENT	WHAT IS IT?	FURTHER INFORMATION
Soya bean flour	These are soya beans that have had the outer coat removed and then ground into flour. Used to thicken foods naturally without adding much flavour. It is also a *gluten*-free alternative flour to wheat flour.	Source of *protein, iron, calcium* and fibre.
Soya bean oil	The soya bean can be processed to extract the natural oils. This oil is used commonly in food manufacturing.	Being a vegetable oil it is a source of *polyunsaturated fat* and is low in saturated fat.
Soya concentrate	This is the same as *soya protein concentrate*.	
Soy(a) lecithin	This is a natural substance derived from *soya beans*. Used in food processing as an *emulsifier*.	
Soya pieces (texturised)	Also called TSP, this is soya flour that has been processed and compressed into chunks or pieces resembling meat. This is often used in meat-substitute dishes suitable for vegetarians.	It is rich in protein and low in *fat*.
Soya protein	This appears when just the protein content of the soya bean has been used.	
Soya protein concentrate	This is when the water and *carbohydrates* have been removed from the *soya bean* to leave a protein-rich (about 70%) substance. It is used in meat products to improve texture and eating quality.	

INGREDIENT	WHAT IS IT?	FURTHER INFORMATION
Soy protein isolate	Same as *soya protein concentrate*.	
Soy sauce	This is a sauce made from puréed soya beans that also contains *salt* and often *wheat flour*. It is used commonly in Asian and Japanese cooking.	
Spaghetti	This is a type of pasta made from *durum wheat* or *durum wheat semolina*.	
Spelt	This is a grain that is an older relative of wheat. It has a higher *protein* content than wheat and contains higher amounts of certain vitamins and minerals. It is not *gluten* free but can sometimes be tolerated better than wheat by sensitive people.	
Spice extract	Spice extract is the essential oil and pigment (colour) in spices; it is used as a natural *flavouring*.	
Spices	A mix of common spices (not pepper and salt, which have to be listed separately). Manufacturers are allowed to use the term 'spices' rather than list each individual one when the ingredient has been used as a flavouring and not for any nutritional benefit.	
Spinach extract	This is used as a natural colour in foods and comes from spinach.	

INGREDIENT	WHAT IS IT?	FURTHER INFORMATION
Spring water	Spring water is collected directly from the spring where it surfaces from the ground and must be bottled at source. It may have been treated to meet standards in pollution. It may be lower in minerals than *mineral water*.	
Spirulina	This is a type of blue-green algae which is sometimes used to naturally colour foods.	
Stabilisers	These are substances which are used to help maintain the texture of products.	
Starch	Added as a *bulking agent*, this is usually derived from a grain. Starch is another name for complex *carbohydrate* or a complex *sugar*.	For more information about carbohydrates and starch see Chapter 3.
Strawberry extract	See *fruit extracts*.	
Strawberry juice from concentrate	See *fruit juice from concentrate*.	
Strawberry purée	See *fruit purée*.	
Stearic acid	A fatty acid found naturally in foods such as beef fat and cocoa beans.	
Stoneground	This is often a term used with *wheat flour* in bread. It basically means that the wheat grain has	

INGREDIENT	WHAT IS IT?	FURTHER INFORMATION
	been ground to a flour using physical action between two stones.	
Sucralose E955	This is a low-calorie sweetener made from real *sugar* (and chlorine) so it tastes like sugar. It is about 600 times sweeter than actual sugar, so it can be used in small quantities and reduce calories whilst still giving a sweet flavour. In the body it cannot be broken down, so provides no energy or calories.	
Sucrose	Another name for the common table *sugar* that we all put in our tea. Used very commonly as a sweetener in foods and drinks. It is generally extracted from sugar cane or sugar beet.	
Sucrose esters of fatty acids E473	This is an *emulsifier* which is derived from *sucrose*.	
Sugar	When sugar is listed on an ingredients label it means that the product contains table sugar that has been added to the product over and above any natural sugars. Sugar comes from two plants, sugar cane and sugar beet. They are processed to extract a substance called *sucrose* (which is another name for sugar). Sugar is a pure *carbohydrate* food. Vitamins and minerals are sometimes present, but only in	Sugary foods and drinks can cause tooth decay, especially when eaten between meals. When you are checking food labels, you can use the following as a guide to what is a lot and what is a little added sugar per 100g food. Look for the 'Carbohydrates (of which sugars)' figure in the nutrition information panel on the label. 15g sugars or more per 100g

INGREDIENT	WHAT IS IT?	FURTHER INFORMATION
	trace amounts. It is used by food manufacturers to help make food taste better. It is found in many sweet and savoury foods, snacks, cereals, drinks, canned foods and ready-meals.	is A LOT of sugar. 2g sugars or less per 100g is A LITTLE sugar. If the amount of sugars is between 2g and 15g per 100g, this is a moderate amount of sugar.
Sugar syrup	This is sugar in a liquid form. It is heated with some water until it dissolves.	
Sulphite ammonia caramel E150d	This is one of four caramel colourants used by food manufacturers ranging from light brown to very dark brown in colour. They are produced by heating *carbohydrates* (e.g. sugars or malt syrups) in the presence of small amounts of food-grade acids, alkalis or salts. These colours are the most commonly used colourants in food. Caramel is also used in *flavourings*.	Research into this food colourant and a link to asthma and skin irritation has not been scientifically conclusive. However, this is one of the food colours the Children's Hyperactivity Support Group recommends is avoided by sensitive children. I found this food colour in just over 60% of the products I looked at which contained food colours.
Sulphites	Sulphur is a naturally occurring mineral found in many different foods in different forms. It is also used by the food manufacturing industry – in the form of sulphates and sulphites – as a number of different food additives to preserve foods. The E numbers are E220 to E228 excluding E225. These are all listed in the guide	By law a packet must declare if a food or an ingredient contained in it has a sulphite content of more than 10mg per 1kg or 1 litre. There is some link between sulphites and asthma and the current Food Standards Agency advice is to avoid sulphite-containing foods if a child suffers from asthma.

INGREDIENT	WHAT IS IT?	FURTHER INFORMATION
	under their individual names with further information. They are used in many foods and drinks such as soft drinks, sausages, burgers, sweets and dried fruit.	This group of additives is also recommended by the Children's Hyperactivity Support Group to be avoided by sensitive children.
Sulphur dioxide E220	This is produced by burning sulphur. It is used in foods as a *preservative*. It is one of the oldest food additives known by man and has been used as a preservative in wine since Roman times. It is a very common preservative in wines and dried fruits as it stops them from discolouring during drying or processing.	Current Food Standards Agency advice is to avoid sulphur dioxide if a child suffers from asthma. This is one of the additives permitted in organic foods.
Sunflower oil	This is a commonly used vegetable oil made from sunflower seeds. It is a source of *omega-6 oils* and is regarded as a healthy oil.	
Sunflower lecithin	This is a natural *emulsifier*, i.e. it helps ingredients to bind together well and is derived from sunflower seeds.	
Sunset yellow E110	This is an artificial *azo dye* food colouring permitted for food use. It gives foods a yellow colour.	This is one of five food colourants which the Food Standards Agency in the UK is currently recommending should be avoided if your child shows symptoms of hyperactivity. For more information see Chapter 2 (Colourings). This is one of the food additives currently under review by the

INGREDIENT	WHAT IS IT?	FURTHER INFORMATION
		European Food Safety Authority. This may lead to a change in regulation sometime in 2008. For updated information about this food dye see the website www.whatsinthis.co.uk. I found it in 5 out of the 570 products I looked at and these were all confectionery items.
Swede	This is a pale-coloured root vegetable that is quite sweet and contains a number of minerals such as calcium and magnesium.	
Sweet potato	This is a relative of the common potato. It has a bright-orange flesh and is sweeter than potatoes, but digests more slowly, giving more longer-lasting energy.	
Sweetened condensed skimmed milk/ sweetened skimmed condensed milk	Condensed milk is cows' milk from which water has been removed and *sugar* added to create a thick, sweet milk. In this case the milk fat has been removed.	

INGREDIENT	WHAT IS IT?	FURTHER INFORMATION
Tahini	This is the name given to the paste when sesame seeds are crushed. It is often found in humuus. It is rich in polyunsaturated *fat*.	
Tapioca starch	Tapioca is a high-*carbohydrate* food that comes from dried cassava (a plant with a root which can be eaten like potatoes, parsnips, beetroots, etc.). The starch, i.e. carbohydrate, is sometimes used in foods as a *bulking agent* as it is pretty flavourless and low in calories.	
Tartaric acid E334	Tartaric acid is found naturally occurring in fruits, in particular grapes. It can be added to foods as an *antioxidant* or to increase the acidity of drinks and conserves.	This additive is permitted in organic foods. For more information about organic foods see Chapter 2 and Appendix 2.
Tetrasodium diphosphate E450 (iii)	This is derived from phosphoric acid and is added to foods as a *raising agent*.	
Textured soya protein	This is a protein which is derived from *soya beans*. It is used as a meat alternative in vegetarian dishes.	

INGREDIENT	WHAT IS IT?	FURTHER INFORMATION
Textured vegetable protein	This is a protein which is derived from vegetables such as peas and potatoes. It is used as a meat alternative in vegetarian dishes.	
Textured wheat protein	This is a protein which is derived from the wheat grain. It comes from the *gluten* part of the wheat grain. It is used as an animal-protein alternative in vegetarian products, as it has a similar texture to meat.	
Thiamin(e)	Also known as *vitamin B1*, it is an essential vitamin involved in helping the body get energy from food. It is found naturally in many foods such as whole grains, meats, fish and pulses. It is used to fortify many foodstuffs, including breakfast cereals and breads.	
Thickeners	These are a group of additives used to thicken the consistency of food. They are used in sauces and gravies, and dressings.	
Titanium dioxide E171	This is a naturally occurring food colouring, which is often used as a white coating or to make something white more opaque. Also used in sunscreens.	
Tocopherol E306	This is natural *vitamin E* and is used as an *antioxidant* in foods.	This may be beneficial for health. This additive is permitted in organic foods. For more

INGREDIENT	WHAT IS IT?	FURTHER INFORMATION
		information about organic foods see Chapter 2 and Appendix 2.
Tomato	When listed in the ingredients as such then it means that whole tomatoes have been used in the food or drink.	
Tomato flavourings	Dried tomatoes are used as a flavouring.	
Tomato paste	This is a thick paste made from tomatoes with the skin and seeds removed.	
Tomato puré	This is when tomatoes have been cooked briefly and then strained to form a thick paste.	
Total cocoa solids	Cocoa solids are the protein and carbohydrate part of the cocoa bean. They contain no *cocoa butter*. White chocolate contains no cocoa solids, just cocoa butter.	Whenever food manufacturers use chocolate in a product they have to list the amount of cocoa solids in percentage form. Higher than 50% is usually found in dark chocolate; up to 30% is usually found in milk chocolate.
Total milk solids	Milk is approximately 86% water and 13% solids, which are made up of the protein, *carbohydrate*, vitamins and minerals found in milk.	
Tricalcium phosphate E341	This is used as an *anti-caking agent* in fine powders such as icing sugar. It is chemically manufactured from calcium phosphate.	

INGREDIENT	WHAT IS IT?	FURTHER INFORMATION
Tripotassium phosphate E340	Potassium salt of phosphoric acid used as an *emulsifier* or *stabiliser* in foods.	
Trisodium citrate E331c	An *acidity regulator*.	
Trisodium diphosphate E450 (ii)	This is a *stabiliser*. It is often found in canned meat and fish.	
Tuna	This is an oily fish.	This provides a source of *omega-3 oils* and protein. For more information about fats see Chapter 3.
Turmeric E100	This is a spice which has a distinctive yellow colour. The yellow pigment is known as *curcumin* and is a permitted natural food colouring.	Also popular in Indian dishes.

INGREDIENT	WHAT IS IT?	FURTHER INFORMATION
Unbleached wheat flour	This means that the wheat flour has not been bleached.	
Unrefined sugar	This is sugar which has not been refined, i.e. has not been processed to remove all impurities.	
Unsweetened	This is a term used when no table *sugar* has been added to a food. It may be used to refer to unsweetened fruits where the sweetness comes only from the natural fruit sugar.	

INGREDIENT	WHAT IS IT?	FURTHER INFORMATION
Vanilla essence	This is an artificial *flavouring*. It is not natural vanilla-pod flavouring.	
Vanilla extract	This is a natural *flavouring* derived from real vanilla pods.	
Vanillin	This is a *flavouring*. It may have been extracted from the vanilla bean but, because this is very expensive, usually a cheaper synthetic one is used. When the word 'vanillin' is used it is synthetic, but if 'vanilla' is listed then it means that the natural form has been used.	Very common flavouring in foods.
Vegetable bouillon	Bouillon is another word for a stock, i.e. where vegetables or meat have been boiled in water and then the stock is either used in this liquid form or it has the water removed from it and becomes a paste or powder form.	
Vegetable carbon/ carbon black E153	This is a black food colouring which comes from burning plant material.	I found this food colouring in 2 products out of 570, which were a cake mix and a variety of confectionery. This is one additive permitted in organic foods. (For more information about organic foods see Chapter 2 and Appendix 2).

INGREDIENT	WHAT IS IT ?	FURTHER INFORMATION
Vegetable extract	This is when a mix of vegetables have been boiled in water and then the stock this creates has been dehydrated (the water has been evaporated) to form a very concentrated substance. Used in vegetable stocks.	An example of a commercial vegetable-extract product is Marmite.
Vegetable fat	This is a fat which comes from a vegetable source e.g. *corn*, *sunflower*, *rapeseed*, *peanut*, soy, *palm*, which is solid at room temperature. Vegetable oil is naturally liquid at room temperature but can be processed to form a solid fat through processes such as hydrogenation.	The refining process removes almost all of the proteins from the oil. Since it's the proteins in foods that can cause allergic reactions, sensitive people probably won't react to refined oil.
Vegetable fibre	This is a natural fibre that is extracted from vegetables and used in the product. This may be to boost fibre content.	
Vegetable glycerine	This is derived from *vegetable oil* (usually *palm oil*) and is used as a *humectant*, as it helps to keep in moisture. It is used in foods to help preserve and prevent foods from drying out, e.g. cakes. It is also used as a base in many soaps.	
Vegetable margarine	This is usually a blend of *vegetable oils* with *emulsifiers*, colours and other ingredients to create a solid butter-like substance that can be used in cooking, especially pastry.	

INGREDIENT	WHAT IS IT?	FURTHER INFORMATION
Vegetable oils	This is a general term for any oil which comes from a plant, e.g. *corn*, *sunflower*, *rapeseed*, *peanut*, soy or *palm*. Vegetable oil is usually a blend of a number of these. It is liquid at room temperature and classed as an unsaturated *fat*. By law, packaged foods must include a list of ingredients. When 'vegetable oil' appears in the list, this can refer to refined oil made from a range of vegetables or other edible plants, but not *olive oil*. The various different oils that make up the vegetable oil don't need to be labelled individually.	Where vegetable oil is in pre-packed food, these oils will have been refined. The refining process removes almost all of the proteins from the oil. Since it's the proteins in foods that can cause allergic reactions, sensitive people probably won't react to refined oils.
Vegetarian cheese	This means that animal rennet has not been used in the processing of the cheese. See *vegetarian rennet*.	
Vegetarian lactose reduced-whey protein concentrate	*Whey* is a liquid formed from milk left over when you make *cheese*. It is used as an ingredient in some foods, as it contains about 1% protein, all the milk lactose and some vitamins and minerals, so it has some nutritional value. It is 92% water. By removing some of the water then the whey becomes concentrated. Milk lactose can also be removed.	
Vegetarian protein	Protein which comes from non-meat or fish origin. Sources include nuts, beans, lentils, chickpeas, grains. *Soya*	

	beans are especially rich in protein and are often used to manufacture meat alternative products such as sausages and burgers.	
Vegetarian rennet	Rennet is used in the process that turns milk into *cheese*. Vegetarian sources are usually bacteria or fungi. Non-vegetarian rennet is of animal origin.	
Vegetarin whey powder	Vegetarian *whey* is a liquid formed from milk left over when you make cheese using *vegetarian rennet*.	
Vinegar	This is a fermented condiment made from sour wine. It is acidic and so used as a *preservative* and also to add flavour to foods.	
Vitamin A	This is an important vitamin for healthy growth and eyesight. There are two types: 1) Retinol which is the animal form of Vitamin A and is found in fish oils, milk, butter, liver and kidneys and 2) Carotene which is the plant source of vitamin A and found in green and orange coloured vegetables and fruits such as spinach and carrots.	For the recommended daily intakes of vitamin A see the table on page 16.
Vitamin B1	An essential vitamin involved in helping the body get energy from food. It is found naturally in many foods such as whole grains, meats, fish and pulses.	For recommended daily intakes see page 16.

INGREDIENT	WHAT IS IT?	FURTHER INFORMATION
	It is used to fortify many foodstuffs, including breakfast cereals and breads. Also known as *thiamine*.	
Vitamin B3	An essential vitamin involved in helping the body get energy from food. It is found naturally in many foods such as red meats, poultry, fish and nuts. It is used to fortify many foodstuffs, including breakfast cereals and breads.	For recommended daily intakes see page 16.
Vitamin B6	An essential vitamin involved in helping the body get energy from food. It is found naturally in many foods such as whole grains, meats, fish, *wheat germ* and *yeasts*. It is used to fortify many foodstuffs, including breakfast cereals and breads.	For recommended daily intakes see page 16.
Vitamin B12	An essential vitamin involved in helping the body get energy from food. It is found naturally in many foods such as dairy products, liver, eggs and shellfish. It is used to fortify many foodstuffs, including breakfast cereals and breads.	For recommended daily intakes see page 16.
Vitamin C	A vitamin and *antioxidant* which is important for a healthy body, healthy skin and healthy immune system. Found naturally in many foods, especially fruit and vegetables. It can also be made artificially.	For recommended daily intakes see page 16.

INGREDIENT	WHAT IS IT?	FURTHER INFORMATION
Vitamin D	This is an important vitamin for bone health as it helps the body to absorb calcium. There is no recommended daily intake for children over 3 years of age if leading a normal lifestyle as the body makes vitamin D naturally from exposure to sunlight. Some foods such as margarines are fortified with vitamin D.	For recommended daily intakes of Vitamin D in under 3s see the table on page 16.
Vitamin E E307, E308, E309	Also known as *tocopherol*, vitamin E is an *antioxidant* and is important for many functions in the body as well as healthy skin. Found naturally in many foods such as *vegetable oils* (wheat-germ oil, sunflower oil), nuts and seeds, and whole grains.	For recommended daily intakes see page 16.

INGREDIENT	WHAT IS IT?	FURTHER INFORMATION
Wheat dextrose	This is a *sugar* found naturally in the wheat grain.	
Wheat fibre	The part of the wheat grain which is rich in fibre is the outer skin (bran and germ layers). These are sometimes added to food to increase the fibre content.	
Wheat flour	The wheat grain is milled to remove the outer shell and leave a fine flour. Where the term 'wheat flour' is used rather than 'wholewheat flour' it means that the wheat grain has been processed. In this some of the fibre and nutrients of the grain have also been removed; this means it is not as nutritious and is also digested more quickly and has a higher *glycaemic index*.	
Wheat germ	This is a part of the wheat grain which is rich in protein and essential vitamins and minerals.	
Wheat gluten	*Gluten* is a binding protein found in a number of grains. Sometimes it is used as a food ingredient to help other	

	ingredients bind together well. In this case the gluten comes from the wheat grain.	
Wheat protein isolate	This ingredient is made from taking the whole wheat grain and removing all the starch to leave a substance which is 90% protein. It is used as an *emulsifier*.	
Wheat starch	A *starch (carbohydrate)* which is removed from the wheat grain. It is used as a *thickener* in foods. It may contain *gluten*, so check labels if necessary.	
Whey	Whey is a liquid formed from milk left over when you make *cheese*. It is used as an ingredient in some foods, as it contains about 1% protein, all the milk lactose and some vitamins and minerals, so it has some nutritional value. It is 92% water.	
Whey powder	*Whey* is a liquid formed from milk left over when you make *cheese*. It is used as an ingredient in some foods as it contains about 1% protein, all the milk lactose and some vitamins and minerals, so it has some nutritional value. It is 92% water. By removing the water content from whey then a powder is produced.	
Whey solids	*Whey* is a liquid formed from milk left over when you make *cheese*. It is used as an	

INGREDIENT	WHAT IS IT?	FURTHER INFORMATION
	ingredient in some foods as it contains about 1% protein, all the milk lactose and some vitamins and minerals, so it has some nutritional value. It is 92% water. The solids are the other 8%.	
Whipping cream	This is natural pure cream which is about 35% fat and can be easily whipped.	
White pepper	Berries which are dried and then ground to a powder. White pepper is produced by removing the outer dark skins from the berries first. Used to add flavour.	
White wine	This is sometimes used to help flavour foods. When wine is cooked the alcohol part of it evaporates, so no alcohol is present in the food.	
Whole egg	This is both egg white and egg yolk.	
Wholegrain	Wholegrain is used on a label when the whole of the grain has been used and nothing has been removed from it. This means the grain still contains all the natural fibres, vitamins and minerals, proteins and starches.	Foods such as breads and cereals made with whole grains or wholegrain flour are usually higher in fibre and nutrients than products that do not use the term 'wholegrain' before listing grains. For more information see Chapter 5.
Wholegrain oats	See *wholegrain*.	
Wholegrain oat flour	See *wholegrain*.	

INGREDIENT	WHAT IS IT?	FURTHER INFORMATION
Wholegrain rolled oats	These are whole oat grains which have been flattened or rolled to leave flakes.	
Wholegrain wheat flour	See *wholegrain*.	
Wholemeal	If the term is used before the word 'flour' then it means that the flour in the product comes from milled *wholegrain* wheat.	
Whole milk powder	Whole full-fat milk which has been reduced to a powder by removing the water content. It still has the same nutritional content of whole milk.	
Whole oranges	This is listed when all of the orange (except the skin), which includes the pith and fibrous part not just the juice, has been used in a product. This means the product contains more of the nutrition and fibre of the orange fruit.	
Whole rolled oats	Oats which have been rolled or flattened.	
Whole rolled wheat	Wheat grain which has been rolled or flattened.	
Whole-wheat flour	This is *wholegrain* wheat that has been milled to a flour. This means that the flour contains all the nutrients and fibre of wholegrain wheat. This will also mean that a food rich	

INGREDIENT	WHAT IS IT?	FURTHER INFORMATION
	in whole-wheat flour will digest slowly and help keep energy levels constant.	
Whole-wheat meal	This is when the whole-wheat grain is ground coarsely and not sifted finely.	
Whole-wheat pasta	This is pasta that has been made using *wholemeal* flour, i.e. the flour has not been processed and still retains the outer skin of the grain, which is high in fibre and rich in nutrients.	

INGREDIENT	WHAT IS IT?	FURTHER INFORMATION
Xanthan gum E415	A natural gum made by bacteria. It is used as a *stabiliser* in foods.	This is a permitted additive in organic foods. For more information about organic foods see Chapter 2 and Appendix 2.

INGREDIENT	WHAT IS IT?	FURTHER INFORMATION
Yeast	This is a living micro-organism used as a *raising agent* in many bakery products.	
Yeast extract	This is when yeast has been processed in a certain way (generally kept secret) to create a food additive which can add or enhance flavour.	
Yogurt	Yogurt is produced from milk by fermenting it with bacteria until it develops a slightly sour flavour. If not stated, then where yogurt is listed in the ingredients list it means full-fat yogurt has been used. This is fine for children.	
Yogurt cultures	These are the live bacteria which can be found naturally in yogurt.	
Yogurt powder	This is when yogurt has had the water removed to form a powder. It still has all the other nutritional properties of yogurt, just without the water.	

INGREDIENT	WHAT IS IT?	FURTHER INFORMATION
Zinc	This is an essential mineral for the body. It plays a role in making enzymes as well as maintaining a healthy immune system. Dietary sources include fish and shellfish, meat such as chicken, wholegrain foods, beans and pulses.	For the recommended daily intakes of zinc see the table on page 16.

NOTES

You may wish to make a note here of any additives you would like your child to avoid or any specific branded products you would like to avoid in future.

E number	Additive Name	Comments

chapter 7

My Findings

INTRODUCTION

This chapter is a summary of the main findings from my analysis of the 570 products, including what you need to be particularly careful about with each product range when choosing either the most nutritionally beneficial or, at least, the best of the bunch. I highlight what surprises I found both in a good way and in not so good ways.

The following information is to be regarded as merely my opinion of the foods I analysed and is not to be taken as being necessarily applicable to all similar products. My opinions should in no way replace your need to look at individual products and make your own informed choices, hopefully with the help of this book.

It must also be pointed out that this information is correct at the time of writing this book, and of course ingredients change, regulations may change and information given on packets can also change.

All of my conclusions stating whether a product should be classed as high in salt, sugar and fat are based on the figures set by the Food Standards Agency and are those used in the Traffic Light labelling system. All are per 100g or 100ml of a product. And remember, red = high, orange = moderate, green = low.

	Salt	Sugar	Fat	Saturated Fat
Red	1.5g or more	15g or more	20g or more	5g or more
Orange	0.3g to 1.4g	5-14.9g	3-19.9g	1.5-4.9g
Green	Less than 0.3g	Less than 5g	Less than 3g	Less than 1.5g

OVERVIEW
Labelling of Nutritional Information

With regards to labelling and the provision of nutritional information such as Guideline Daily Amounts (GDAs) and Traffic
Light labelling I found that GDAs were cited on over 60 per cent
of the products. Though useful, the GDAs are often not given for
children. Learning that a product or a portion provides 4 per
cent of an adult's daily recommended amount of sugar does not
really make it easy to decide whether it is a product you want
to buy for your child.

When GDAs were listed for children they were all based on
five- to ten-year-olds, so you will need to mentally adjust these
a little if your child is older or younger.

The Traffic Light system was found on only about 10 per
cent of the products (particularly breads). This is a shame
as in my opinion the Traffic Light system is much easier to
understand and enables you to make an informed choice in
seconds.

Hydrogenated Fat
The 25 products I found to contain hydrogenated fat were mainly
items such as cakes, biscuits, chocolate bars and the odd cereal
bar. I didn't find any in ready-meals, which I was pleasantly
surprised about.

Cheap Frozen Foods
A big surprise was that almost all of these contained no artificial colours or flavourings and far fewer preservatives than
expected. On many occasions these products outshone more
expensive ranges with regards to artificial additives and salt
content. There was not always a significant difference in the

contents of other ingredients either, for example quantity of meat. You heard it here first!

Ingredients Lists

The main negative point I had here was that these lists are often so small that even the very trained eye would have difficulty assessing a product based on this in under ten minutes!

Children's Ranges

The foods looked at here were those aimed only at children and state this clearly on the packet. Due to the lack of specific legislation for these types of products it is left to the individual manufacturers and retailers to decide what guidelines are used when creating these ranges. I found that on the whole the specific ranges developed by a number of the large retailers are, in the main, excellent. However, there are always some that are a little higher in salt or sugar than is ideal, and they are not necessarily additive-free (though many of the flavours and colours used are natural).

One negative point about these ranges is that only one out of five I looked at included GDA information for children on the package. Therefore, it is still very necessary to check individual packets.

Own Brands

These are retailers' own ranges. I found that there seems to be little difference between these and well-known brands in many cases. Some products I looked at contained fewer ingredients than the more expensive well-known brand equivalents and some were better labelled with information such as GDAs and Traffic Light labelling.

Value Brands

Again, many of these so-called value/economy ranges seemed to differ very little in their ingredients compared to the more expensive brands. Some contained fewer ingredients. However, with some product ranges the value/economy products did clearly contain cheaper ingredients or lower amounts of key ingredients such as meat or fish. In one or two cases, particularly with drinks, these ranges contained more artificial colours.

Yogurts

I looked at a total of 29 yogurts and yogurt drinks, including 20 specifically marketed to children. I looked at a mix of yogurt tubes (popular for lunchboxes) and fruit yogurt and fromage frais selection packs. I also looked at four varieties that claimed to have no added sugar as well as six organic varieties.

Only three of the products I looked at included information about GDAs, of which two gave children's GDAs. Fourteen of the products included children's characters on the packaging.

Out of 29 products, almost half of them (fourteen) contained added food colours though only two of these contained artificial food colours. Nineteen products contained added flavourings (ten of which listed natural flavourings), whilst four of the products contained preservatives.

The key nutrient to watch out for in this product range seems to be the sugar content. Only four products did *not* contain added sugar and three products would be classed as high in sugar (more than 15g per 100g) with the other 25 being classed as moderately high in sugar (5–15g of sugar per 100g). All yogurts, of course, contain the naturally occurring sugar lactose, so even natural yogurt contains approximately 6g per 100g, but look for sugar contents above this amount to get an idea of added sugar. As noted in Chapter 3 of the book, a good way of looking at the sugar content of a product is to think of it in terms of teaspoons: 1 teaspoon = 5g.

Almost half the yogurts had 'Contains real fruit' or 'Contains real fruit purée' on the package. The average fruit content of these was 6 per cent, which does not seem particularly high, and certainly would not go far in replacing an item of fresh fruit. This seems to be used as a marketing tool rather than an indicator of the actual nutritional benefits of the product.

Breakfast Cereals

I looked at 25 different breakfast cereals, including many aimed at children (ten included cartoon characters on the packaging). I looked at a range of the frosted and chocolate cereals as well as those with added fruits and honey, and also some which are marketed as wholegrain.

A significant number of mainstream cereals are clearly aimed at children but have no special information for parents, such as children's GDAs. Out of the 25 cereals I looked at 18 had GDA information for adults and only two had GDA information for children.

Again, the main nutrient to check carefully is the sugar content, which is often very high. Out of the products sampled, twenty would fall into a 'high in sugar' category (i.e. more than 15g of sugar per 100g), a further three would be regarded as medium (between 5g and 15g) and only two were low in sugar (less than 5g).

The other nutrient that is often higher than ideal for children is the salt content. Three had a high salt content (i.e. more than 1.5g salt/0.6g sodium per 100g) and only four had low salt contents (less than 0.3g salt/0.1g sodium). The rest would be classed as having medium salt contents.

Just over half of the cereals contained added flavourings.

On the positive side, 24 out of 25 were low in fat and saturated fat.

None contained preservatives and five contained food colours (all natural).

Bread and Bakery Products

I looked at fifteen items in this range, which included breads (wholemeal, white, brown, half-and-half, and own-brand as well as well-known brands) and bakery items such as rolls, pitta breads, pancakes, muffins and crumpets.

This product range seemed to be labelled with the Traffic Light system more than some of the other ranges, with six of the products (40 per cent) using it. Thirteen of the products included GDA information but only two of these also included children's GDA information.

Salt is added to bread as it acts as an important raising aid. However, the amounts added to 75 per cent of the breads I looked at would mean that such breads would be classed as high in salt. Every Traffic Light label provided was coloured red for salt.

The main difference between wholemeal and brown bread seems to be that for wholemeal bread wholemeal flour is always listed as the first (highest) ingredient and for brown bread the first ingredient is wheat flour (and often wholemeal flour does not appear in the ingredients). Wholemeal flour is naturally richer in fibre and a number of vitamins and minerals than wheat flour (wheat flour is wholemeal flour that has been further processed). In the brown-bread items I looked at bran or wheat germ was usually added to the bread to make it richer in fibre and give it the brown colour. Brown bread, therefore, is not the same as wholemeal bread.

Six of the fifteen products contained preservatives (usually calcium propionate E282), which is added to inhibit mould growth.

Ready-Meals

I looked at a total of eighty ready-meals. Of these, 39 were specific to children and 41 were ones marketed at the whole family. Ready-meals have had a very bad press over the last few years so I was very surprised to find that overall this product range was very good.

The key nutrients to look out for in this range are fat and salt, though even here over 70 per cent would be classed as low in saturated fat and only 20 per cent would be classed as high in salt. Only eight contained any preservatives and four contained food colours (though all of these were natural ones).

The only addition a parent might want to make to some of them is adding a portion of extra vegetables.

My findings seem to show that parents can find a number of large retailers offering own-brand children's ranges of ready-meals that are very suitable for children and certainly wouldn't have a negative impact on a child's health if consumed once or twice a week. Good news for all us busy parents and carers!

Dried Fruit, Fruit and Cereal Snack Bars

I looked at a total of 32 products in this group, which included child snack-size packets of dried fruit, 100 per cent dried-fruit bars and fruit and cereal bars. Of those I looked at, 80 per cent were specifically aimed at children in some way through the use of cartoon characters and/or the wording 'ideal for lunch-boxes' on the packaging.

Probably due to limited space on packaging, only six included GDA information on the packet and of these only one listed children's GDAs.

The key ingredient to watch for with these types of products is sugar. Of the 32 products, 18 had added sugar in the form of table sugar, honey and/or rice syrups. The other fourteen did not contain any added sugar but, as they contained dried fruit, they contain naturally occurring fruit sugar.

I also found eight products that, though they contained no added sugar, contained added fruit-juice concentrates used to make a product taste sweeter.

It can be quite misleading for parents to read the claim 'No added sugar' and 'Zero added sugar' on these products as it could lead you to assume the product could be classed as low in sugar. This is not the case. Every single product I looked at would be classed as high in sugar (i.e. over 15g of sugar per 100g) though for many of these products this sugar has not been added but is found within the actual ingredients (i.e. dried fruit). The benefits of dried fruit over sugar are many: dried fruit contains a number of valuable vitamins and minerals as well as some fibre, which added sugars generally do not, and (also importantly for children) dried fruit is not as harmful for teeth as added sugar.

If as a parent you would like to limit the overall intake of sugar in your child's diet for any reason, including dental health or if you have very young children, bear in mind that these products, though they offer some nutritional benefits, should be seen as quite high in sugar and it may be wise for them not to be used as regularly in a child's diet as fresh fruit.

With regards to additives, six products contained added colours, though only one was not natural. Eleven contained added flavourings, though six were natural. Seven products contained the preservative sulphur dioxide (E220), which is worth noting if your child suffers from asthma or may be sensitive to additives.

Sweets and Confectionery

I looked at a total of fifty products, including a range of chocolate bars, lollies and sweets. Most of these are well-known brands, but I also looked at a few own-brand items.

Only fourteen products included GDA information on the packaging and only two listed children's GDAs. This is probably often down to limited space on the packaging.

The key ingredients to watch for are fat (including saturated fat) and sugar content (though sweets usually do not contain any fat but are very high in sugar). This means these products should be given to children as a 'treat' rather than a regular part of their diets.

Almost none of the products in this group can really claim to have any nutritional benefits for the body other than providing lots of calories, sugar and possibly also fat.

From an additives perspective, 21 contained food colours. Five of these contained azo dyes including quinoline yellow E104, sunset yellow E110 and carmoisine E122, which are currently under safety review by the European Food Safety Authority (EFSA) following the results of a research study indicating a link between these particular azo dyes and a negative impact on children's behaviour. Only four contained preservatives (sugar is a natural preservative, which is maybe why) but these four all contained sulphites – worth noting if your child may be sensitive to these. Thirty-eight contained added flavourings (only two of which stated they were natural flavourings).

Many items of own-brand confectionery I looked at contained no artificial colours or flavourings.

Drinks

I looked at a total of 33 products in this group, which included some concentrated squash/cordials, ready-diluted cartons of these, fruit juices, flavoured water, fruit-smoothie drinks and well-known fizzy soft drinks. Of these ten had 'No added sugar' on the label. I looked at a mix of own-brand, well-known brands, organic and economy ranges.

Eleven products included GDA information on the packaging (three of which listed children's GDAs). Two of the products had Traffic Light labelling on them.

As a group of products I found drinks one of the most difficult to pick through and assess how suitable or healthy they were for children. Many of the products were very high in sugar and most of those with no added sugar contained artificial sweeteners, such as aspartame E951 (5 of 33 products), sodium saccharin E954 (5 of 33 products) and acesulfame K E950 (5 of 33 products). Some contained both added sugar and artificial sweeteners. In favour of sweeteners they are non-cariogenic, i.e. they are not unhealthy for children's teeth in the same way both sugar and fruit acids can be.

This group of products also contained more preservatives than any other product range I looked at. This may be because many of them are 'No added sugar' or 'Sugar free' products so they do not benefit from the natural preservative action of sugar and need to have preservatives added to them. Over a third (13 out of 33) of the products contained preservatives and of these five contained the preservative sodium benzoate (E211). Sodium benzoate is currently under safety review by the EFSA following the results of a research study indicating a link between this and particular azo dyes with a negative impact on children's behaviour. Seven of the products contained sulphites. This is important to note if your child suffers from asthma and hyperactivity.

Regarding colours, twelve of the products contained added food colours but only three of these contained artificial ones. One surprise was how many of the products contained added flavourings, 24 out of 33 products. Of these products only nine used natural flavourings.

A number of the products I looked at have clever marketing ploys and claim to contain real fruit juice and a range of added vitamins and minerals. However, on closer inspection many only contained 10 per cent fruit juice, the rest being made up of water, some artificial sweeteners and the added vitamins. I felt that this stretched my personal definition of 'good for my child' somewhat.

There are some good fruit juices and fruit smoothies out there that contained only 100 per cent fruit or fruit juice and nothing else, and a small glass of these would count as one item of fruit for your child. However, don't forget that these are best drunk with meals rather than outside of meal times as this is healthier for children's teeth.

Current advice by the British Dietetic Association is that for all children under four years any cordials and fruit juices need to be diluted well with water.

Cakes and Biscuits

I looked at a total of fifty products in this group, including some of the cakes and biscuits that have been around since I was a child (back in the 1970s). I looked at a mix of products marketed specifically at children as well as a number of family favourites. I included some more expensive ranges, some own-brand ranges and some value ranges. Quite a few of those I looked at highlighted on the packaging that they were suitable for lunchboxes as they were individually wrapped in child-size portions.

About half of the products (24) included information on GDAs but only six gave children's GDAs. Only one product had Traffic Light labelling.

The key nutrients to look out for are the pretty obvious fat, saturated fat and sugar contents of these types of foods – which is the reason they taste so good! One of the common things I found is that portion sizes are quite big for young children and the fat and sugar contents can be reduced significantly if you halve or even cut a cake into quarters for your child. This means they could still enjoy a 'treat' without taking in too many calories from fat and sugar. The other less positive thing about this range of products is that they don't really contain any ingredients that can supply children with beneficial nutrients such as vitamins and minerals. It would be very easy for a child to fill up on these products or consume a significant proportion of their daily suggested calorie intake but to fall very short on actual vitamins and minerals, as well as nutrients such as protein and healthy fats.

This product range was where I saw hydrogenated fat listed in the ingredients, more so than in any product range (twelve out of fifty products).

With regards to additives, twenty-one of the fifty products contained added food colours. Of these eight contained artificial azo dyes: including quinoline yellow E104, sunset yellow E110 and carmoisine E122, all of which are currently under safety review by the EFSA (as mentioned above in Sweets and Drinks).

Where cherries or marshmallows are used these are usually accompanied by two artificial food colourings. When cherries are processed they lose their colour, so this is often added back to them in the form of erythrosine E127. I also found cochineal E120 in every product that contained marshmallows. I found sixteen products contained preservatives and 35 of the fifty products contained added flavourings (only twelve of which listed natural flavourings).

Having said this, there were 25 products that contained no colours or preservatives, but only seven that contained no colours, preservatives or flavourings.

Cake Mixes

I looked at a total of nine products, which included some own-brand products.

If your child suffers from sensitivity to food colours then you will need to check the packaging carefully. Of the nine products, eight contained food colourings and of these four contained azo dyes (between four and six azo dyes in each product) including quinoline yellow E104, sunset yellow E110, carmoisine E122, allura red E129, all currently under safety review by the EFSA (see above).

All of the nine products contained added flavourings, but only one product listed natural flavourings.

Puddings

I looked at a total of 25 different puddings, from traditional family puddings such as fruit crumble and custard and rice pudding, to children's puddings like jelly, Angel Delight and chocolate dessert pots.

The key nutrients to watch out for seemed to be fat and sugar. All the products I looked at would be classed as high or medium in sugar and a third of them would be classed as high in fat (all of which were also high in saturated fat). Therefore, these types of foods should be given to children as occasional treats.

With regards to additives, fifteen of the 25 products contained colours but all of these except two products were natural. Two of the products out of 25 contained azo dyes (and one of these contained Carmoisine E122, currently under safety review by the EFSA). Every single one of the products I looked at contained added flavourings (seven were natural flavourings). None of the products I looked at contained preservatives even though there was a mix of fresh puddings, frozen puddings and packet ones. Five of the products contained added sweeteners though only two of them were sugar-free products.

Savoury Snacks

I looked at a total of eighteen products, which included many well-known crisps, some of the premium-brand and own-brand crisps, other savoury snacks such as breadsticks and baked snacks, as well as organic puffed snacks produced especially for young children.

The main nutrients to watch out for seemed to be salt and fat (including saturated fat). Some of the crisps contain over 30 per cent fat. All but three of the products I looked at would be regarded as high in salt (i.e. over 1.5g of salt per 100g).

Regarding additives, six of the products contained food colours (though all of these were natural) and three of the products contained preservatives (all of these were sodium metabisulphite E223), worth noting if your child may be sensitive to sulphites. Of the eighteen products, half of them contained added flavourings (only two were listed as natural) and six contained the flavour enhancer monosodium glutamate (E621).

Lunchbox Items, Sandwich Fillers, Cheese Products
I looked at a total of 35 products, which included some of the popular lunchbox fillers like cheese and dips, some of the cheese, meat and biscuit packs, a range of cheeses in different shapes and sizes aimed at children, and cheese spreads and a few sandwich-filler items from jars of paste to fresh spreads.

The key nutrient to watch out for with this group of products is salt. Out of 35 products, 32 (over 90 per cent) would be classed as high in salt (over 1.5g of salt per 100g of product) and the other three would be regarded as having a medium salt content. Considering that these types of products are aimed very specifically at children and are very popular with them this should be of concern to parents.

The other nutrient that is always going to be high in cheese products, whether just plain old natural cheese or processed, is the fat content and the saturated fat content. However, this is of less concern to parents of children under five years of age, and with children over five cheese is still an important potential source of both calcium and protein in a child's diet. Cheese shouldn't be eaten in unlimited quantities as this would raise the intake of saturated fat in the diet, but is fine as part of a balanced healthy diet.

With regards to labelling this was the product range that had most labelling aimed at children, for example 10 out of 35 listed children's GDAs.

With regards to additives just under a third of the products contained added colours, but these were all natural. Preservatives were slightly more common, however, with a third of the products containing them. Five products contained the preservative sodium nitrite (which were those products that included cured meats such as ham). Three of the products I looked at contained the flavour enhancer monosodium glutamate and eight contained added flavourings.

With this group of products I saw many nutrition and health claims on the packaging centred around calcium. Some have even added further calcium to the product to provide a significant amount (I saw up to 33 per cent) of a child's RDA of calcium per portion.

Quite a few of the products contained processed cheese rather than 'natural' cheese and some felt it necessary to make a claim of their containing 'real cheese', though this is sometimes only 18 per cent.

Meat

I looked at a total of 52 products in this group, which included a mix of cooked meats popular for children's sandwiches and fresh and frozen meat items aimed at children or popular with children (e.g. chicken nuggets, breaded chicken breasts, goujons, burgers and sausages). I looked at more expensive and organic varieties as well as economy-range items. I also looked at some ready-to-roast meat joints.

The main nutrient to watch out for is salt, which would be classed as high in over 70 per cent of the products I looked at. The main differences between some of the brands and products were the actual meat contents and that some products use re-formed meat. Many had water and starches added. This meant that many of the products were not very good-quality proteins.

All of the cooked meats contain preservatives of some kind, which are obviously important to help keep the product safe for consumption. I found three that contained sulphites (sodium metabisulphite E223) and ten that contained nitrites. Most of the fresh and frozen meat products did not contain preservatives.

Only 17 per cent of the products included information about GDAs on top of the nutritional information and only five listed children's GDAs, even though over 80 per cent of the products I looked at were aimed mainly at children.

Fish Products

I looked at twelve fish products, which included fresh and frozen fish pieces in breadcrumbs and batter, and fishcakes. Seven out of the twelve products were ones aimed specifically at children and the others were marketed at the whole family.

My first observation was not very positive as I saw actual fish contents ranging between 35 and 63 per cent. The products with the highest fish content were not always the obvious ones and some of the cheaper frozen varieties seemed to fare well. Therefore I would advise not making assumptions based on price and brand but checking individual products carefully. The higher the fish content then the better-quality source of protein provided by that product for your child.

The key nutrient to watch out for seems to be salt. Of the twelve products, three would be classed as high in salt (more than 1.5g of salt per 100g) and the other nine would also fall into the moderately high category (between 0.3g and 1.5g).

Potato Products

I looked at thirteen products including oven chips, frozen potato shapes, potato wedges, waffles, croquettes, French fries and roast potatoes.

Overall, this product range proved to be healthier than I had expected. Many of the products contained only potatoes and sunflower oil. Some of the products have added salt, which can be quite high (they would be classed as moderately high – between 0.3 and 1.5g of salt per 100g) but others contained no added salt.

The fat content was low (less than 3g per 100g) for two of the products and the rest would be classed as moderate (between 3g and 20g).

None of the products I looked at contained any preservatives or flavouring, and only one contained food colouring (which was natural).

The main difference between these products and eating boiled new potatoes or a jacket potato is that they tend to be lower in fibre, as the potato skins have been removed. This also means they are probably lower in vitamins and minerals than whole potatoes, as many of these are found just underneath the skin. Two of the products, however, did have the skins on them. Processing will also have some effect on the vitamin and mineral contents.

Ice Cream and Lollies

I looked at a total of fifteen ice creams and lollies, which included plain vanilla ice creams, premium products, frozen yogurt-style puddings, children's lollies and ice-cream cone and choc ices.

Two-thirds of the products did have adult GDA information on them but only two had children's GDAs.

The main nutrients to look out for in this product range were sugar and fat. Lollies contained lots of added sugar and all would be classed as high-sugar products (more than 15g per 100g). The ice creams were also high in sugar – all would be classed as high in sugar. The ice-cream products also contained some fat and all but one I looked at would be classed as moderately high in fat.

With regards to additives none of the products I looked at contained any preservatives. Every single one contained added flavourings but over half of these were natural. All but two products contained food colours but all of these were natural.

Tinned Food, Jars of Ready-Made Sauces and Packet Meals

The majority of the 31 products in this category were tins and ready-made pasta sauces in jars and pouches. The tins included items such as baked beans, spaghetti hoops, ravioli, macaroni cheese, hot dogs and meatballs.

Even though 80 per cent of the products are aimed towards children (with Disney-type characters on the packaging or forming part of specific children's ranges) only 9 out of 31 had adult GDAs and none included any children's GDAs. None of the products had Traffic Light labelling on them.

Overall this was one of the healthiest ranges I looked at, with none of the products being classed as high in salt, sugar or fat. In fact, all the products would be classed as low in sugar, half the products were low in fat (less than 3g per 100g) and all were classed as moderate for salt contents. These are clearly not unhealthy products for children, but they do contain some salt so shouldn't be eaten too frequently, and they are not necessarily sources of many nutrients valuable for children.

With regards to additives about a third contained colours, but these were all natural except one. If your child is sensitive to monosodium glutamate then check the packets as three of the products contained this. Only two products contained any preservatives, which were sodium nitrites and sulphites. Of the low-sugar-style products (e.g. low-sugar baked beans) only one contained added sweeteners.

Condiments, Spreads, Sauces, Jams

I looked at a total of sixteen products in this category, which included a range of margarines and dairy-free spreads, jams, peanut butters, Marmite, chocolate spreads, gravy, salad creams and products like tomato ketchup.

Only two contained GDA information and one gave children's GDAs. None of these products had Traffic Light labelling.

The main nutrients to watch for with the spreads and condiments is salt – half would be classed as high in salt. Sugar is the main nutrient to watch for in jams, but also in many of the condiments such as tomato ketchup.

With regards to additives about half of the products contained food colours but these were all natural. Only two of the products contained preservatives.

Many of the spreads were high in polyunsaturated fats, which are healthier for us than the saturated fats found in butters, and many were also enriched with a number of vitamins and minerals (e.g. vitamins A and D, folic acid and vitamin B12).

Vegetarian Foods

I looked at a total of four meat-alternative products such as meat-free burgers, sausages and chicken-nugget-style products. Of course, many of the products I looked at in the other ranges are suitable for vegetarians.

Looking specifically at processed-meat alternatives, I found that the ones I looked at contained very few additives, only food colours, and these were natural.

Regarding salt and fat content they would all be classed as moderately high in these (though low in saturated fat).

Children's Medicines

I looked at seven children's medicines, noting their sugar and additive contents rather than their active pharmaceutical ingredients. Of these two were 'sugar free' varieties. I also looked at a mix of ibuprofen and paracetamol-based products as well as cough medicine and teething preparations.

It must first be noted that medicines may need to contain added sugar to disguise the taste of the medicine, and that adding colours has been done to encourage children to take them.

I found that all seven products were sweetened with sweeteners rather than sugar. Those that were sugar-free had been sweetened with non-calorific intense sweeteners and the others with bulk sweeteners. For more information about sweeteners see Chapter 2.

With regards to food colourings, three of the products I looked at contained food colourings. All of these were azo dyes and two of the products contained the artificial food colours quinoline yellow E104, sunset yellow E110 and carmoisine E122. All of these colours are currently under safety review by the EFSA (see earlier under Sweets and Drinks). There may be some changes to food regulation about the use of these colours sometime in 2008 – whether there will be any similar change to legislation of children's medicines remains to be seen.

Medicines tend to lag behind foods with trends such as changing food colours and sweeteners. It is a lot harder to reformulate a medicine than a food and it takes much longer to develop, as they are regulated differently and more stringently than foods. Even a small change in the type of food colour used requires complete testing and trials that are time-consuming and very expensive.

I found three of the products contained preservatives, all of which were from the benzoate group of preservatives (E214, E216, E218).

Medicines do have to legally list warnings about the possible link between ingredients and allergic reactions.

Information on Additives and E Numbers

WHAT DO FOOD ADDITIVES ACTUALLY DO?
This chapter provides a quick and simple explanation for many of the roles carried out by additives.

Acidity Regulators
These are substances that help control the level of acidity in a food or drink. For example, they help maintain the sharp acidic flavour of lemonade.

Anti-Caking Agents
These stop powder items from forming into clumps.

Antioxidants
Antioxidants help prevent foods going rancid or discolouring when exposed to oxygen.

Bulking Agents
Found in many products, bulking agents can help add bulk to foods without adding lots of calories.

Colourings
There are three types used in foods:
• Natural colours often derived from plant and insect extracts
• Inorganic pigments derived from metals
• Synthetic azo dyes

Emulsifiers
Oil and water do not naturally mix well. An emulsifier is a substance that is added to help them mix.

Emulsifying Salts
These are substances that are added to foods to keep them stable and keep them firm and 'together'.

Firming Agents
These are used to retain firmness and crispness in products even when they are processed. Many foods contain natural firming agents (e.g. pectin in apples).

Flavour Enhancers
These help perk up the flavour of a product. They do not have any characteristic flavour of their own, but when added to foods they act to enhance the flavour of that food.

Flavourings
These are substances used to give flavour and/or smell to a product. There are natural ones, nature-identical ones, synthetic (man-made) ones and smoke flavourings. The specific flavouring used in a product does not have to be listed under current EU legislation. There are over 2,500 flavourings currently permitted in food use. Under EU legislation the expression 'natural flavourings' can only be used on those extracted from vegetable or animal materials.

Flour Treatment Agents
These help to keep white flour white and make a flour less 'strong' and so more suitable for cake baking than bread making.

Gelling Agents
These are substances which when added create a gel-like texture.

Glazing Agents
These give food an appetising shiny surface. They may sometimes also have a protective role.

Humectants
These help to absorb moisture from a food, and in doing so help to stop the growth of mould.

Packaging Gases
These are gases that are pumped into the packaging of products to stop them going brown (e.g. ready-prepared salads).

Preservatives
These are a large group of additives that help to keep food safe to consume for longer. They have a number of roles, from stopping the growth of harmful bacteria and fungi to stopping foods from going rancid. They include the group of preservatives known as sulphites and benzoates. Natural preservatives include salt, sugar and vinegar.

Raising Agents
These include familiar substances like baking powder (sodium bicarbonate) that help foods such as bread and cakes to rise, and are used for home baking as well as in the manufacturing industry.

Sequestrants
There are sometimes traces of metals naturally present in foods. These metals can reduce the shelf life of a product, i.e. they speed up foods going off. Sequestrants are used for their

ability to attach themselves to these metals and make them inactive.

Stabilisers
These are substances that are used to help maintain the texture of products.

Sweeteners
There are two types of sweeteners used in foods and drinks. First are the 'intense' sweeteners, which are used in very tiny amounts and are usually many hundreds of times sweeter than sugar. They provide the body with no calories. Second are bulk sweeteners, which are used to replace sugar and are not harmful for teeth but do provide some calories.

Thickeners
These are substances that help to thicken a food and are used in foods like sauces, condiments, gravies and dressings. They are often derived from plants.

COMPLETE E NUMBERS LIST
A list of all current E numbers and the additive names listed under the key headings.

E Number	Name
Colours	
E100	Curcumin
E101 (i)	Riboflavin
E101 (ii)	Riboflavin-5'-phosphate
E102	Tartrazine

E104	Quinoline yellow
E110	Sunset yellow FCF; Orange yellow S
E120	Cochineal; Carminic acid; Carmines
E122	Azorubine; Carmoisine
E123	Amaranth
E124	Ponceau 4R; Cochineal red A
E127	Erythrosine
E128	Red 2G
E129	Allura red AC
E131	Patent blue V
E132	Indigotine; Indigo carmine
E133	Brilliant blue FCF
E140	Chlorophylls and chlorophyllins
E141	Copper complexes of chlorophyll and chlorophyllins
E142	Green S
E150a	Plain caramel
E150b	Caustic sulphite caramel
E150c	Ammonia caramel
E150d	Sulphite ammonia caramel
E151	Brilliant black BN; Black PN
E153	Vegetable carbon
E154	Brown FK
E155	Brown HT
E160a	Carotenes
E160b	Annatto; Bixin; Norbixin

E160c	Paprika extract; Capsanthian; Capsorubin
E160d	Lycopene
E160e	Beta-apo-8'-carotenoic acid (C30)
E160f	Ethyl ester of beta-apo-8'-carotenoic acid (C30)
E161b	Lutein
E161g	Canthaxanthin
E162	Beetroot red; Betanin
E163	Anthocyanins
E170	Calcium carbonate
E171	Titanium dioxide
E172	Iron oxides and hydroxides
E173	Aluminium
E174	Silver
E175	Gold
E180	Litholrubine BK
Preservatives	
E200	Sorbic acid
E202	Potassium sorbate
E203	Calcium sorbate
E210	Benzoic acid
E211	Sodium benzoate
E212	Potassium benzoate
E213	Calcium benzoate
E214	Ethyl p-hydroxybenzoate

E215	Sodium ethyl p-hydroxybenzoate
E218	Methyl p-hydroxybenzoate
E219	Sodium methyl p-hydroxybenzoate
E220	Sulphur dioxide
E221	Sodium sulphite
E222	Sodium hydrogen sulphite
E223	Sodium metabisulphite
E224	Potassium metabisulphite
E226	Calcium sulphite
E227	Calcium hydrogen sulphite
E228	Potassium hydrogen sulphite
E230	Biphenyl; diphenyl
E231	Orthophenyl phenol
E232	Sodium orthophenyl phenol
E234	Nisin
E235	Natamycin
E239	Hexamethylene tetramine
E242	Dimethyl dicarbonate
E249	Potassium nitrite
E250	Sodium nitrite
E251	Sodium nitrate
E252	Potassium nitrate
E280	Propionic acid
E281	Sodium propionate
E282	Calcium propionate

E283	Potassium propionate
E284	Boric acid
E285	Sodium tetraborate; borax
E1105	Lysozyme
Antioxidants	
E300	Ascorbic acid
E301	Sodium ascorbate
E302	Calcium ascorbate
E304	Fatty acid esters of ascorbic acid
E306	Tocopherols
E307	Alpha-tocopherols
E308	Gamma-tocopherols
E309	Delta-tocopherols
E310	Propyl gallate
E311	Octyl gallate
E312	Dodecyl gallate
E315	Erythorbic acid
E316	Sodium erythorbate
E319	Tertiary-butyl hydroquinone (TBHQ)
E320	Butylated hydroxyanisole (BHA)
E321	Butylated hydroxytoluene (BHT)
E586	4-Hexylresorcinol

Sweeteners	
E420 (i)	Sorbitol
E420 (ii)	Sorbitol syrup
E421	Mannitol
E950	Acesulfame K
E951	Aspartame
E952	Cyclamic acid and its sodium and calcium salts
E953	Isomalt
E954	Saccharin and its sodium, potassium and calcium salts
E955	Sucralose
E957	Thaumatin
E959	Neohesperidine DC
E962	Salt of aspartame-acesulfame
E965 (i)	Maltitol
E965 (ii)	Maltitol syrup
E966	Lactitol
E967	Xylitol
E968	Erythritol

Emulsifiers, Stabilisers, Thickeners and Gelling Agents	
E322	Lecithins
E400	Alginic acid
E401	Sodium alginate
E402	Potassium alginate

E403	Ammonium alginate
E404	Calcium alginate
E405	Propane-1,2-diol alginate
E406	Agar
E407	Carageenan
E407a	Processed eucheuma seaweed
E410	Locust bean gum; Carob gum
E412	Guar gum
E413	Tragacanth
E414	Acacia gum; Gum arabic
E415	Xanthan gum
E416	Karaya gum
E417	Tara gum
E418	Gellan gum
E425	Konjac
E426	Soybean hemicellulose
E432	Polyoxythelene sorbitan monolaurate; Polysorbate 20
E433	Polyoxythelene sorbitan mono-oleate; Polysorbate 80
E434	Polyoxythelene sorbitan monpalmitate; Polysorbate 40
E435	Polyoxythelene sorbitan monostearate; Polysorbate 60
E436	Polyoxythelene sorbitan tristearate; Polysorbate 65
E440	Pectins

E442	Ammonium phospatides
E444	Sucrose acetate isobutyrate
E445	Glycerol esters of wood rosins
E460	Cellulose
E461	Methyl cellulose
E462	Ethyl cellulose
E463	Hydroxypropyl cellulose
E464	Hydroxypropyl methyl cellulose
E465	Ethyl methyl cellulose
E466	Carboxy methyl cellulose; Sodium carboxy methyl cellulose
E468	Crosslinked sodium carboxy methyl cellulose; Enzymatically hydrolysed carboxy methyl cellulose
E470a	Sodium, potassium and calcium salts of fatty acids
E470b	Magnesium salts of fatty acids
E471	Mono-and diglycerides of fatty acids
E472a	Acetic acid esters of mono-and diglycerides of fatty acids
E472b	Lactic acid esters of mono-and diglycerides of fatty acids
E472c	Citric acid esters of mono-and diglycerides of fatty acids
E472d	Tartaric acid esters of mono-and diglycerides of fatty acids
E472e	Mono-and diacetyltartaric acid esters of mono-and diglycerides of fatty acids
E472f	Mixed acetic and tartaric esters of mono- and diglycerides of fatty acids

E473	Sucrose esters of fatty acids
E474	Sucroglycerides
E475	Polyglycerol esters of fatty acids
E476	Polyglycerol polyricinoleate
E477	Propane-1,2-diol esters of fatty acids
E479b	Thermally oxidised soya bean oil interacted with mono and diglycerides of fatty acids
E481	Sodium stearoyl-2-lactylate
E482	Calcium stearoyl-2-lactylate
E483	Stearyl tartrate
E491	Sorbitan monostearate
E492	Sorbitan tristearate
E493	Sorbitan monolaurate
E494	Sorbitan mono oleate
E495	Sorbitan monopalmitate
E1103	Invertase

Others

Acid, acidity regulators, anti-caking agents, anti-foaming agents, bulking agents, emulsifying salts, firming agents, flavour enhancers, flour treatment agents, foaming agents, glazing agents, humectants, modified starches, packaging gases, propellants, raising agents and sequestrants.

E260	Acetic acid
E261	Potassium acetate
E262	Sodium acetate

E263	Calcium acetate
E270	Lactic acid
E290	Carbon dioxide
E296	Malic acid
E297	Fumaric acid
E325	Sodium lactate
E326	Potassium lactate
E327	Calcium lactate
E330	Citric acid
E331	Sodium citrates
E332	Potassium citrates
E333	Calcium citrates
E334	Tartaric acid (L-(+))
E335	Sodium tartrates
E336	Potassium tartrates
E337	Sodium potassium tartrate
E338	Phosphoric acid
E339	Sodium phosphates
E340	Potassium phosphates
E341	Calcium phosphates
E343	Magnesium phosphates
E350	Sodium malates
E351	Potassium malate
E352	Calcium malates
E353	Metatartaric acid

E354	Calcium tartrate
E355	Adipic acid
E356	Sodium adipate
E357	Potassium adipate
E363	Succinic adipate
E380	Triammonium citrate
E385	Calcium disodium ethylene diamine tetra-actetate; calcium disodium EDTA
E422	Glycerol
E431	Polyoxyethylene (40) stearate
E450	Diphosphates
E451	Triphosphates
E452	Polyphosphates
E459	Beta-cyclodextrin
E500	Sodium carbonates
E501	Potassium carbonates
E503	Ammonium carbonates
E504	Magnesium carbonates
E507	Hydrochloric acid
E508	Potassium chloride
E509	Calcium chloride
E511	Magnesium chloride
E512	Stannous chloride
E513	Sulphuric acid
E514	Sodium sulphates

E515	Potassium sulphates
E516	Calcium sulphates
E517	Ammonium sulphate
E520	Aluminium sulphate
E521	Aluminium sodium sulphate
E522	Aluminium potassium sulphate
E523	Aluminium ammonium sulphate
E524	Sodium hydroxide
E525	Potassium hydroxide
E526	Calcium hydroxide
E527	Ammonium hydroxide
E528	Magnesium hydroxide
E529	Calcium oxide
E530	Magnesium oxide
E535	Sodium ferrocyanide
E536	Potassium ferrocyanide
E538	Calcium ferrocyanide
E541	Sodium aluminium phosphate
E551	Silicon dioxide
E552	Calcium silicate
E553a (i)	Magnesium silicate
E553a (ii)	Magnesium trisilicate
E553b	Talc
E554	Sodium aluminium silicate
E555	Potassium aluminium silicate

E556	Aluminium calcium silicate
E558	Bentonite
E559	Aluminium silicate; Kaolin
E570	Fatty acids
E574	Gluconic acid
E575	Glucono delta-lactone
E576	Sodium gluconate
E577	Potassium gluconate
E578	Calcium gluconate
E579	Ferrous gluconate
E585	Ferrous lactate
E620	Glutamic acid
E621	Monosodium glutamate
E622	Monopotassium glutamate
E623	Calcium diglutamate
E624	Monoammonium glutamate
E625	Magnesium diglutamate
E626	Guanylic acid
E627	Disodium guanylate
E628	Dipotassium guanylate
E629	Calcium guanylate
E630	Inosinic acid
E631	Disodium inosinate
E632	Dipotassium inosinate
E633	Clacium inosinate

E634	Calcium 5'-ribonucleotides
E635	Disodium 5'-ribonucleotides
E640	Glycine and its sodium salt
E650	Zinc acetate
E900	Dimethylpolysiloxane
E901	Beeswax, white and yellow
E902	Candelilla wax
E903	Carnauba wax
E904	Shellac
E905	Microcrystalline wax
E912	Montan acid esters
E914	Oxidised polyethylene wax
E920	L-Cysteine
E927b	Carbamide
E938	Argon
E939	Helium
E941	Nitrogen
E942	Nitrous oxide
E943a	Butane
E943b	Iso-butane
E944	Propane
E948	Oxygen
E949	Hydrogen
E999	Quillaia extract
E1200	Polydextrose

E1201	Polyvinylpyrrolidone
E1202	Polyvinylpolypyrrolidone
E1204	Pullulan
E1404	Oxidised starch
E1410	Monostarch phosphate
E1412	Distarch phosphate
E1413	Phosphated distarch phosphate
E1414	Acetylated distarch phosphate
E1420	Acetylated starch
E1422	Acetylated distarch adipate
E1440	Hydroxyl propyl starch
E1442	Hydroxyl propyl distarch phosphate
E1450	Starch sodium octenyl succinate
E1451	Acetylated oxidised starch
E1452	Starch aluminium octenyl succinate; Polyethylene glycol 6000
E1505	Triethyl citrate
E1518	Glyceryl triacetate; triacetin
E1520	Propan-1,2-diol; propylene glycol

Further Useful Information

ADDITIVES CURRENTLY PERMITTED IN ORGANIC FOODS

At the time of writing there are 47 food additives permitted in organic foods under current EU legislation.

E Number	Name	Function and Permitted Uses
E153	Vegetable carbon	Natural food colouring permitted for use in two named cheeses: Ashy goat cheese, Morbier cheese.
E160b	Annatto; bixin; norbixin	Natural food colouring permitted for use in four traditionally coloured cheeses: Red Leicester, Double Gloucester, Scottish Cheddar, Mimolette cheese.
E170	Calcium carbonate	Acidity regulator. Shall not be used for colouring or calcium enrichment of products.
E220 Or E224	Sulphur dioxide Potassium meta-bisulphite	Preservative. Only allowed for use in fruit wine and cider and smaller amounts allowed than for non-organic alcoholic drinks.
E250 Or E252	Sodium nitrite Potassium nitrate	Preservative. Only allowed for use in the curing of bacon and ham. Specified maximum residual amounts.
E270	Lactic acid	Acidity regulator and preservative.

E290	Carbon dioxide	Natural gas used to produce carbonated water and soft drinks.
E296	Malic acid	Acidity regulator and preservative.
E300	Ascorbic acid	Antioxidant. For use only in meat products.
E301	Sodium ascorbate	Antioxidant. For use only in meat products in connection with nitrates or nitrites.
E306	Tocopherol-rich extract	Antioxidant for fats and oils.
E322	Lecithin	Emulsifier and/or lubricant. To be used only in milk products.
E325	Sodium lactate	Antioxidant. To be used in milk-based and meat products only.
E330	Citric acid	Preservative.
E331	Sodium citrate	Acidity regulator.
E333	Calcium citrate	Preservative.
E334	Tartaric acid (L(+)-)	Preservative.
E335	Sodium tartrates	Emulsifier.
E336	Potassium tartrates	Raising agent for flour.
E341(a)	Monocalcium phosphate	Raising agent allowed only in self-raising flours.
E400	Alginic acid	Stabiliser. Only to be used in milk-based products.
E401	Sodium alginate	Stabiliser. Only to be used in milk-based products.
E402	Potassium alginate	Stabiliser. Only to be used in milk-based products.

E406	Agar	Thickener/gelling agent. Only to be used in milk-based and meat products.
E407	Carrageenan	Stabiliser/thickener/gelling agent. Only to be used in milk-based products.
E410	Locust bean gum	Thickener/gelling agent.
E412	Guar gum	Thickener.
E414	Arabic gum	Stabiliser.
E415	Xanthan gum	Stabiliser.
E422	Glycerol	Primarily a humectant. Used only in plant extracts.
E440 (i)	Pectin	Thickener. Only to be used in milk-based products.
E464	Hydroxypropyl-methylcellulose	Can only be used to make vegetarian capsules.
E500	Sodium carbonate	Acidity regulator. Only to be used in 'dulce de leche' and soured cream butter.
E501	Potassium carbonate	Raising agents in flour, also acidity regulators.
E503	Ammonium carbonate	Raising agent.
E504	Magnesium carbonates	Neutraliser and buffer. Only to be used in milk coagulation.
E509	Calcium chloride	Allowed only as a carrier where vitamins and minerals are required by law in flour or as a coagulation agent in tofu.

E516	Calcium sulphate	Allowed only as a carrier where vitamins and minerals are required by law in flour or as a coagulation agent in tofu.
E524	Sodium hydroxide	Very limited use: allowed in specific products and processing.
E551	Silicon dioxide	Anti-caking agent in herbs and spices.
E553b	Talc	Use only as a coating agent for meat products.
E938	Argon	Natural inert gas.
E939	Helium	Natural inert gas.
E941	Nitrogen	Natural inert gas.
E948	Oxygen	Natural inert gas.

Useful Contacts and Further Information Sources for Parents

THE 'WHAT'S IN THIS?' WEBSITE
www.whatsinthis.co.uk

Visit the website for more information on the following:

- Full list of references used in writing the book
- Updates on food and additives legislation
- Updates on new ingredients and additives
- Contact Clare Panchoo

OTHER USEFUL WEBSITES

1. Food Standards Agency website – www.food.gov.uk and www.eatwell.gov.uk

2. The Food Commission – www.foodcomm.org.uk

3. FAO/WHO website on food standards and guidelines – www.codexalimentarius.net

4. Asthma UK – www.asthma.org.uk

5. The British Thoracic Society – www.brit-thoracic.org.uk

6. The National Eczema Society – www.eczema.org

7. Children's Hyperactivity Support Group – www.hacsg.org.uk – website plus printed material resources

8.   The Soil Association – www.soilassociation.org

9.   Action on Additives – www.actiononadditives.com

10. Organix Foundation – www.organixfoundation.org

11. British Nutrition Foundation – www.nutrition.org.uk

12. British Dietetic Association – www.bda.uk.com

13. The Caroline Walker Trust (an organisation dedicated to the improvement of public health through good food) – www.cwt.org.uk

14. Allergy UK – www.allergyuk.org

15. Vegetarian Society – www.vegsoc.org

16. Vegan Society – www.vegansociety.com

17. Coeliac Society – www.coeliac.co.uk

Index